D0073535

The Celluloid Courtroom

The Celluloid Courtroom

A History of Legal Cinema

Ross D. Levi

Westport, Connecticut
London

Library of Congress Cataloging-in-Publication Data

Levi, Ross D., 1967–
The celluloid courtroom : a history of legal cinema / Ross D. Levi.
p. cm.
Includes bibliographical references and index.
ISBN 0-275-98233-5 (alk. paper)
1. Justice, Administration of, in motion pictures. 2. Lawyers in motion pictures. I. Title.
PN1995.9.J8L48 2005
791.43'6554—dc22 2004028024

British Library Cataloguing in Publication Data is available.

Library of Congress Catalog Card Number: 2004028024
ISBN: 0-275-98233-5

First published in 2005

Praeger Publishers, 88 Post Road West, Westport, CT 06881
An imprint of Greenwood Publishing Group, Inc.
www.praeger.com

Printed in the United States of America

The paper used in this book complies with the Permanent Paper Standard issued by the National Information Standards Organization (Z39.48-1984).

10 9 8 7 6 5 4 3 2 1

To my teachers . . .

who whether in writing, film or the law taught me to see the world with new eyes, especially two who passed on during the writing of this book: Mr. Rick Kravet and Dr. Murray Yaeger.

And to my greatest teachers,
my Mom and Dad.

Contents

Acknowledgments

For film credit information contained throughout this book, I occasionally referred to Castell, Ron, ed. *Blockbuster Video Guide to Movies and Video 1995*. New York: Dell Publishing, 1994; Halliwell, Leslie. *Halliwell's Film Guide*. 7th ed. New York: Harper & Row, 1989; but most especially to the International Movie Database (IMDb), which can be accessed at http://www.imdb.com. It is an invaluable resource, so comprehensive that to pass it over in favor of any reference book would be folly. As a consequence, the IMDb should rightfully be relied on as the reference source for movie credits contained herein that I did not gather directly from the films themselves or, in some cases, for confirmation of credit information in a more easily accessed format. I also utilized http://www.lawyer-jokes.us for the great jokes at the beginning of Chapter 4. Trust me, it was difficult to pick only a few.

On a personal note, I would like to express my gratitude to my friend and former intern, Eric Lichtenfeld, who started me on the path to this book and who always kept me thinking more deeply about film. Eric, when you left me you were but a learner, now you are the master.

I would also like to pay tribute to two late, great artists: Fred Ebb, the lyricist of such wonderful musicals as *Chicago*, which is discussed in this book, and whose death made the newspapers the day I handed in my manuscript; and Vito Russo, author of *The*

Celluloid Closet, the seminal work on gay cinema that inspired the title for this book.

Thanks are also due to Jack Spillum, Beldeen Fortunato, Rich Redlo, and Peter Hanson, who shared their experience and expertise in helping this rookie author navigate the unfamiliar world of for-profit publishing.

Speaking of publishing, my appreciation goes to my editor, Eric Levy, for his guidance, patience, and confidence.

Thanks to Michael Meade for helping to rekindle my writing spirit.

Thanks to Barry Gast for keeping me computer equipped and technologically up to date.

Kudos to Bob & Ron's and The Buttery for always keeping me well fed.

Thanks to my colleagues at the Empire State Pride Agenda, past and present, for always being supportive of my outside activities and to all my comrades in the lesbian, gay, bisexual, transgender, and greater civil rights movement for providing inspiration and for always setting the bar for achievement so high. Thanks also to my former colleagues in the film industry, especially Penny Costigan, who helped expand my knowledge and love of the movies.

Finally, of course, thanks to my friends and family for being understanding about the missed social opportunities and the phone calls and e-mails that were sacrificed for my writing, and for always being my champions, especially my immediate family—Mom and Dad, LeeAnn, Kevin, and Quinton; my extended family in Connecticut, New York, Pennsylvania, Florida, and elsewhere; Jim and Brian; the QAF boys in Albany, including Mark, James, Jim, Tony, Michael, Rob, and the Frat House; Cleve and Jack; the Clark-Suarez's; the Chilver-Ziskind's; the Ringwood Lake crew—Wayne, Rich, and Michael; the gang from B.U.; and my dear Paul.

Introduction: Making the Case

When a film lover is asked to identify a favorite type of film, the genre of legal cinema is likely to go completely unmentioned. Comedy, drama, action, romance, science fiction, horror, westerns, musicals, and even documentaries are all more likely to be identified long before someone would profess a love for films involving America's legal system, but start any group discussing the topic of legal films, and even the most casual filmgoer will begin throwing out dozens of titles including at least one or two that invoke a passionate response (e.g., "Oh my God, Atticus Finch is everything a man should be!"). It is rare to find a person without a favorite legal film, and yet probably no one has ever complained that there is not a legal film section at the local Blockbuster Video.

Why this conspicuous absence of the legal film from our culture's cinematic consciousness? Clearly it is not for a want of entries from which to choose. Our legal system has been a central player in hundreds of films since the birth of the talkie and has been utilized for every dramatic effect from pathos to humor. As just one illustration of the ubiquity of legal cinema, a search of the very comprehensive on-line International Movie Database (IMDb) reveals 366 American, English-language films with plot descriptions that contain the word "lawyer," 251 that mention "judge," and 50 with "jury."[1] Even taking into account the duplicate film titles in each search result, the devotee of legal films clearly has a bounty of selections in which to indulge. Yet even with this embarrassment of cinematic riches, there is no category on the IMDb's list of movie genres for legal or courtroom films. Ditto for the *Blockbuster Video Guide to Movies and Video*.[2]

It also cannot be argued that the impact of the legal film has been too insignificant to manifest itself in our collective cultural awareness. There are plenty of legal films, as well as characters and phrases from those films, that have firmly planted themselves in our pop culture consciousness. When someone demands to be told the truth on some matter, expect some joker to repeat Jack Nicholson's phrase from the witness chair in *A Few Good Men*: "You can't handle the truth!" Likewise, if someone is accused of being out of order, expect the rebel to respond as Al Pacino did in *. . . And Justice for All* by saying, "You're out of order! You're out of order! The whole trial is out of order." Serving as a more scientific example of the cultural impact of legal film, players in the legal system showed up as five of the fifty greatest heroes identified in an American Film Institute 2003 survey of cinematic heroes and villains—a full 10%, second as a represented profession only to detectives and other law enforcers.[3] The number one hero, in fact, was a lawyer: the aforementioned Atticus Finch in *To Kill a Mockingbird*. It is worth noting that one of the criteria AFI used for judging a hero was his or her cultural impact, defined as whether the character has "made a mark on American society in matters of style and substance."

At least one of the reasons for this pervasive lack of legal cinema visibility, as compared to, say, the horror film, musical, or western, must be the difficulty in defining the genre. Film genres are identified mostly by their conventions—those settings, characters, plot lines, wardrobe, objects, or even music that are common to all the films of that genre. For example, the presence of a horse, particularly one ridden by a man wearing a cowboy hat, usually indicates that the film is a western. Likewise, singing and dancing signal that a film is a musical, a dark figure ominously wielding a knife is a denizen of the horror movie or thriller, fatigues are the dress of the war movie, and so on.

Legal cinema, in contrast to these other quickly recognized genres, is not nearly so easily identifiable. There is not really any common characteristic, no unifying convention that could be found in every movie that should probably be considered a "legal film." For example, if we require legal films to have a lawyer as a prominent character, we leave out films that focus on the jury, such as *Twelve Angry Men*, *The Juror*, and *Jury Duty*. Requiring a courtroom or at least a courthouse to be the setting for at least one scene in the legal film would exclude the films that have something important to say about lawyers or our legal system but do not do so in front of a judge. One such example is *The Firm*, a movie almost exclusively about lawyers and a legal case without having a single scene in a courtroom. There does not even need to be a legal case involved in a film for it to contain some commentary on how the law and officers of the court shape our society. For example, it is significant that Robert De Niro's flawed character in Irwin Winkler's *Night and the City* is a lawyer, yet the closest he gets to the law is breaking it when he purchases a fraudulent liquor license for his girlfriend, played by Jessica Lange.

There is not even a commonly accepted term for films that have as their central concern a legal matter or someone intimately involved with the legal system. "Courtroom drama," a fairly familiar term and one with clearer conventions and identifiers, is far too limiting to encapsulate the entire genre of films involving the legal system and the players within it. For one thing, the "courtroom drama" label would exclude a whole range of legal films that are not strictly dramas, from legal thrillers like *The Pelican Brief* to courtroom comedies like *Adam's Rib*, *My Cousin Vinny*, and *Liar Liar*, to even what might be dubbed legal horror, such as *The Devil's Advocate*; legal western, such as *The Life and Times of Judge Roy Bean*; and legal musical, as personified in the Academy Award's Best Picture of 2002, *Chicago*. It would also disqualify the aforementioned court films without a court, such as *The Firm*.

Ironically, as difficult as it is to define the legal cinema genre broadly enough to encapsulate all films with a strong legal component, it is equally difficult the limit the genre. Is every film with a lawyer or a court scene a "legal film"? For example, *The Untouchables* concludes with a dramatic courtroom sequence where Al

Capone is finally sent to jail for tax evasion, thanks to the work of Kevin Costner's Eliot Ness. But could that modern gangster film be considered part of legal cinema? Likewise, *JFK* also has a trial as its climax, culminating in a courtroom sermon by, again, Kevin Costner—this time as New Orleans District Attorney Jim Garrison, dramatically imploring the jury and, through it, the nation, "Don't forget your dying king." (Perhaps Kevin Costner is a convention of the nonlegal courtroom film.) The courtroom in *JFK*, however, is mainly a convenience allowing director and cowriter Oliver Stone to summarize the hundreds of pieces of conspiracy evidence that have been dropped throughout the over two and a half hours of story before the film's third-act courtroom sequence even begins. The courtroom gimmick also allows what could have been a tedious litany of conspiracy evidence to be presented in a dramatic, efficient, and believable way. Even with the legal element as the climax of the film and the whole movie being basically about the preparation for a criminal prosecution, one would be hard pressed to find a *JFK* viewer who characterized the film as one about lawyers or our legal system.

It is probably not enough to say that, like Justice Stewart's famous quote about pornography from *Jacobellis v. Ohio*,[4] we know a legal film when we see one. As previously discussed, we cannot rely on the device used to signal most other film genres—the convention—because the expected conventions in legal films (e.g., the courtroom, the lawyer, a verdict, etc.) are, on one hand, absent in a number of prominent legal films and, on the other hand, present in a number of films that would not rightly be classified as full-fledged members of legal cinema. In legal terms, this would make such a definition both under- and overinclusive. That leaves us with a quandary: We all have some sense of what a legal film is, but how shall we define it?

Perhaps the most relevant criteria for deciding how to define the genre of legal cinema is whether a film has something to say about the way Americans view their legal system and the players within it. While moviegoers rely on genre to choose their entertainment, the main importance of genre to critics and scholars is what the genre and its evolution say about society. By relying on the way society's view of its legal system is affected by the film to qualify the movie as part of legal cinema, we need not worry about whether there are courtrooms, lawyers, a verdict, or even a legal case anywhere in the film. We include films like *The Devil's Advocate*, which leaves a definite impression about lawyers but has very little courtroom action, and exclude films like *What's Up Doc?*, which has a brief courtroom sequence as its comic climax but makes no real impact on the viewer regarding our legal system.

This "cultural impact" criterion will also naturally and appropriately put the heaviest emphasis on films that appear to be purposefully making a statement about our legal system. In this way, we intentionally create a pecking order of legal films, with the top tier being reserved for films that intend to be about the legal system or at least law, order, or justice, and that in fact have some success in changing the viewer's perception of that system. The bottom tier will contain films that may have a plot point or character involved in the legal system, but in a way that is almost incidental. For example, the adult Peter Pan, portrayed by Robin Williams in Steven Spielberg's *Hook*, was probably made a lawyer not as a statement on lawyers but to emphasize that Peter has become what he most loathed: the very model of a responsible, grown-up man. Clearly, Spielberg had no intention of changing the audience's view of lawyers, as evidenced by the fact that Peter's occupation is never mentioned after the first half of the film. Quite the contrary, rather than trying to change the audience's opinion of lawyers, Spielberg probably used the lawyer stereotype to make the audience "tsk-tsk" in a Pavlovian way at the cold, ruthless character Peter had become. Subconsciously, the connection is made: Peter Pan used to be so free and innocent and now, horrors, he's a lawyer! One character says as much when reacting to Peter's career as a mergers and acquisitions lawyer: "So, Peter, you've become a pirate." Although there will be occasions when this portrayal of a stereotype will affect society's perception of the legal system, if nothing else by reinforcing it, *Hook* is an example of a film that uses the stereotype of the lawyer in a brief, insignificant way for its own purposes and leaves the institution of the law neither harmed nor repaired.

This is not to say that only the serious or satiric film that delves into the law is the one that will most affect society's view of the legal system and can thus most properly lay claim to its place in legal cinema. Sometimes, what is meant to be just a compelling thriller or a laugh-out-loud comedy may in fact affect an audience's perception of a lawyer, judge, or jury more than would a film that is a thinly disguised editorial comment on the law. Clearly, *... And Justice for All* has an esteemed place in legal cinema as an up-front, if heavy-handed, commentary on the state of America's criminal justice system, at least in the late 1970s. Films, however, like *My Cousin Vinny* and *Legally Blonde*, which probably had no higher aspiration than being solid fish-out-of-water comedies, also have a significant effect on society's view of what an attorney should be or how an attorney should act. It is entirely possible that these two humble comedies expanded the audience's view of what makes a lawyer tick at least as much as, if not more than, a serious message movie like *... And Justice for All.*

Of course, the films that are most likely to affect audiences are the ones that attempt to both comment on the legal system *and* provide a compelling or moving story. *Philadelphia* had a wide cultural impact when it was released in 1993, winning Tom Hanks his first Academy Award and providing him the opportunity in his Oscar acceptance speech to talk about compassion and tolerance. The audience cried at the plight of Hanks's Andy Beckett as he fought both AIDS and the injustice of being fired from his law firm for being gay. The story, the most prominent portrayal up until that time in a high-profile Hollywood film of a gay man and a person with AIDS, would have probably captivated audiences even without the legal component. The fact that the film also drew the ironic and disturbing conclusion that the keepers of the law were not above ignoring it out of fear and prejudice only increased the film's effect. In this way, because it was both an involving human story and a statement on our legal system, *Philadelphia* can lay its claim to being one of the more established members of the cinematic bar.

After the film that comments on the legal system while telling a powerful human story, the next type of film most properly considered legal cinema is the film that highlights the fallible human elements in the players involved in a legal system that society likes to think of as impartial and institutional. *Inherit the Wind* is a film solidly about an actual trial, the so-called Scopes monkey trial, but it is the passion of Spencer Tracy and Fredric March's opposing counsels, each a true believer on opposite sides of the debate around evolution versus creationism, that holds and speaks to the audience. The film's effect on society's view of the legal system comes not so much from the trial subject matter but from the zealotry of lawyer Matthew Harrison Brady (the stand-in for the real-life William Jennings Bryan) and the righteousness of opposing counsel Henry Drummond (the alter ego of Clarence Darrow). Likewise, although *Twelve Angry Men* is exclusively about the final phase of a criminal trial, namely, the deliberations of a jury as it tries to reach a unanimous verdict, it is the dramatic interaction of the anonymous jurors, spurred by their biases, convictions, aspirations, and life experiences, that makes the audience question the efficacy of being judged by a jury of one's peers. The effect on the audience's view of America's legal system comes not from the trial that is the subject of the film but from the human foibles that insert their way into the supposedly impartial judicial process.

Films without any, or with extremely little, specific trial action, such as *The Firm* and *Erin Brockovich*, might rightly squeeze their way into legal cinema under this "human foible" criterion. Because both these films have much to say about how greed and power can corrupt the legal system, they surely leave the audience questioning whether America's legal system is all that it is cracked up to be. Whether this type of film is an extension of the second tier of legal films—those showing human weaknesses or strengths as affecting the legal process—or a slightly lower third tier that makes a similar statement, albeit outside the context of a trial, is immaterial at this point. Suffice it to say that films that place an emphasis on how the human element affects the legal system, even absent a specific trial or courtroom element, will have a prominent place in legal cinema.

So let us define the universe of our study of legal cinema. Our examination of legal cinema shall be limited to American, English–language films that intend to present some commentary on America's criminal or civil legal system, or at least have the effect of leaving a significant impression with the viewer about the efficacy of the adversarial legal process or the players within it. The highest order of these films is likely to be those that either tell a compelling human story while presenting commentary on the legal system, or that tell a legal story that emphasizes how the human condition either helps or hinders the quest for justice that is presumably the basis for having a legal system in the first place.

We should recognize that our parameters for legal cinema exclude a number of significant films that have a strong legal or courtroom component. For example, we will not be looking at any of the films dealing with foreign legal systems, such as *Dry White Season* (which involves a trial in South Africa), either of the cinematic adaptations of Kafka's *The Trial* (dealing presumably with the French legal system), or the movie of Agatha Christie's play *Witness for the Prosecution* (with pivotal scenes in a British courtroom). We also leave out adjudicative systems that are not part of either the mainstream criminal or civil court system, such as the court martial proceeding that is the focus of *A Few Good Men*, *A Soldier's Story*, and *Breaker Morant* (doubly disqualified, as it involves a foreign court martial in Australia) and the war crimes tribunal portrayed in *Judgement at Nuremberg*. Although any of these films might have an effect on an American audience's view of its legal system, such an effect would be a matter of audience confusion because the proceedings being portrayed are outside of the legal system established to dispense justice to the general American population. Furthermore, to focus on these films would be to lessen the emphasis where it would be most effectively placed: on those films that either intend or that could be reasonably expected to directly leave even the casual moviegoer pondering America's system of civil and criminal litigation.

We should also be explicit that in our focus on legal cinema we are consciously excluding films that deal less with the legal system but more expansively with the greater justice system. When we speak of America's legal system as analyzed in legal cinema, we are speaking of the process from when a criminal defendant is charged with a crime, or the party to a civil action seeks representation, up through the verdict, perhaps including sentencing in the criminal context. We are not including the components of the entire justice system that occur before and after this period, such as the law enforcement or criminal investigation phases of the justice system that get the legal system involved in the first place, nor the incarceration or punishment period, which is mostly the law taking its course after a verdict has been reached.

This distinction between the legal system and the justice system is widely understood, if not often articulated. For example, the punishment following the trial process is generally referred to as an element of the criminal *justice* system, not the legal system. Similarly, as the narration that opens every episode of the television program *Law & Order* reminds us, the criminal investigation is an equally important half of the criminal justice system, with the other, separate half being the criminal prosecution. It is an appropriate distinction because "legal" connotes and denotes the application of the law; justice, in turn, takes over in the administration of that law. The difference is also illustrated in two separate comments from Christopher Lloyd's Judge Doom in *Who Framed Roger Rabbit?*, who characterizes fear of a guilty verdict as "respect [for] the law" but characterizes his literal liquidation of toon characters in a chemical dip as "dispensing of justice."

We must admit, however, that this line between "justice" films and "legal" films is more blurred than we might desire. For example, films like *Dead Man Walking* and *The Green Mile* question whether the death penalty can ever be a just result in a flawed justice system. Likewise, the "innocent man convicted" motif in films like *An Innocent Man*, *The Fugitive*, *Shawshank Redemption*, and to some degree, *Running Man* and *Minority Report*, question the effectiveness of a legal system that results in the wrong man being punished. Both these types of film may take place after the legal portion of the criminal justice system has been completed but nonetheless are likely to influence an audience's opinion of their legal system. Would they then rightly be part of legal cinema under our definition?

Thankfully, our definition of "legal system" as the adjudicative, litigation portion of the larger justice system gives us guidance. Films like *Dead Man Walking* and even *Shawshank Redemption*, which opens with a brief trial sequence, may very well get viewers wondering about how fair America's justice system, including the legal system, may be, but neither of these films is very likely to get us thinking about judges, lawyers, or juries. Whatever condemnation they may have is for the entire justice system from beginning to end, and although that may include the legal system at least in part, the film is only a relevant part of legal cinema if it focuses on the legal system specifically and examines the legal system at least as much as it examines the justice system as a whole. For example, *The Green Mile* implies that racial prejudice had a part in the wrongful arrest, charging, and conviction of an innocent man now sitting on death row, but the fairness of his trial is never seriously brought into question. Audience members would be reasonable to infer that the impartiality of the jury might be suspect, but that implication is never clearly made. Even if it were, it would be in the context of an entire justice system—indeed, an entire culture steeped in racism. In this way, the audience's view of the legal system is not nearly as shaken as its view of the justice system as a whole. Thus, although *The Green Mile* would rightly be categorized as a film dealing with justice, and perhaps even America's criminal justice system, it could not accurately be called a legal film that implicates the legal system more than any other component of the greater whole.

There will be films, however, in which the justice system and legal system meet head on, thus allowing those films to be rightly classified as legal cinema. *The Hurricane*, for example, involves the appeal of Rubin "Hurricane" Carter, wrongfully convicted and serving a life sentence. Because the film includes the legal appeal of Carter, the justice system's punishment portion is hauled back into the courtroom, thus re-invoking the legal system. It is a legal film because it focuses specifically on a legal matter, not simply the punishment outcome of a legal trial. Likewise, *Murder in the First* is mostly a prison film focusing on the cruel punishment of Henri Young. It becomes a legal film, however, once the young lawyer played by Christian Slater mounts a defense claiming that the punishment Young was exposed to on Alcatraz Island twisted him into a maniacal murderer. Both these films start as movies focusing on the greater justice system but reenter the legal system, and thereby legal cinema, by using the adjudicative process specifically to try the justice system itself.

Our legal argument is now firmly crafted: We are prepared to look at those films that have affected our society's view of its legal system. Our legal strategy will be to break down the major players in that system—the client, judge, jury, and lawyer—and to see how their portrayals have changed over the course of cinematic history. We will give as our legal summation some thoughts on why the often-unnoticed genre of legal cinema is nonetheless so completely pervasive throughout cinema as a whole, and why the legal system lends itself so well to Hollywood representation.

Lights . . . the parties are represented by counsel, and the jury has been impaneled. Camera . . . the judge is entering the courtroom as the bailiff prepares to make his announcement: "All rise! Court is now in session." And . . . action!

1

The State versus . . . : The Client

"A lawyer is not supposed to become personally involved with his client. But there are all kinds of lawyers, and all kinds of clients, too."
—Matt Damon as Rudy Baylor in *The Rainmaker*

In the end, for all the bells and whistles of the legal process, it is all supposed to be about the client. The legal system exists not to ponder theoretical questions of justice but exclusively to deal with the suspected misstep of a person accused of a crime or to address the grievance of a person trying to be made whole by the outcome of a civil suit. Countless lawsuits have been dismissed for failure to show any real harm to a client. On these occasions, when a court is being asked to make a decision about what amounts to only a hypothetical matter, it will steadfastly refuse to get involved. Even the U.S. Supreme Court has declined to decide cases after finding that the party or parties petitioning the court failed to show any real harm. In one well-known example, a divorced father challenged whether his child should be expected to say "under God" every day in school as part of the Pledge of Allegiance. The Court refused to decide the underlying constitutional question, finding instead that the father was not harmed sufficiently to have standing to even bring the case because he had custody of his daughter only a few days a month. One might wonder whether the justices used the requirement of harm as an excuse to dodge a controversial question regarding the separation of church and state, particularly when several lower courts were satisfied as to standing and able to decide the case on its merits. Still, the principle was clearly underscored that without a client whom the court believes has been tangibly damaged, the legal system will decline to spring into action, and no trial will occur.

This is not to say that that there is unanimous agreement in legal circles about how central the client should be to his or her own representation. Some lawyers see themselves as the professional who knows best. They would no more seek a client's opinion on litigation strategy than an electrician wiring a house would seek the opinion of the contracting home owner on what grade of wire to use. Some clients (especially corporate clients) even prefer this model, with the lawyer almost exclusively dealing with legal issues so that the client can attend to more important matters, such as running a business. Other lawyers swear by a "client-centered" approach in which the client is included as a full partner in the litigation. This lawyer takes the term "representation" quite seriously and tries to act only as an extension of the client by explaining options in legal strategy as they arise and letting the client chose the path that best suits his or her goals.

Even with this question of how large the role of the client should be in the lawyer/client relationship, however, even the most arrogant lawyer would have to admit that the client is a vital component of the legal process. The more God-like attorney might view the client as a necessary evil—a sentiment that might be shared by the clients in these arrangements in regard to their affection for their lawyers. In contrast, more touchy-feely, client-centered lawyers might view the client as God. However, all must agree that the whole thing makes little sense without the presence of an accused or aggrieved client.

Vital, however, does not equal prominent, and all in all, society seems to have far more interest in all the other players in the legal system than in the client, who is supposed to be the focus of the whole thing in the first place. Celebrities on trial notwithstanding (i.e., trials involving people who are already celebrities before the subject of their legal matter even occurs), the client is often relegated to the role of bit player in the public's recollection of legal milestones. Lawyers and lay people alike who can quote passages from *Brown v. Board of Education* or who are at least familiar with the concept of "separate but equal" immortalized through the case are likely to have difficulty providing any details about Mr. Brown, the parent who sued so that his daughter could attend the legally segregated all-White public school near his home. Almost everyone has heard of Clarence Darrow or F. Lee Bailey or Johnnie Cochran, but how many people know that the name "Jane Roe," the plaintiff in *Roe v. Wade*, was fictional to protect the anonymity of the woman suing for her right to have a legal abortion? And although the names of famous justices like Brandeis and Cardozo become immortalized in many ways (including in the names of institutions of higher learning), clients usually become little more than a convenient way to refer to a legal principle. Brown and Roe, for example, have become much less people than concepts, as when someone discusses "the importance of *Brown*," or "the meaning of *Roe*."

Should we be surprised, then, that the vast majority of the hoopla in legal cinema is about everything but the client? The audience is more likely to take pleasure in (or have disdain for) the sly maneuverings and clever repartee of the attorneys, or to thrill as the lawyer doggedly seeks out witnesses and evidence to get ever closer, step by step, to the ultimate truth. The client often must be content to be the plot device that gets the action going or the sympathetic window dressing to give the lawyer the high-stakes reason to win the case.

Just a reading of the marquee shows the priority that Hollywood places on the client: While the lawyers are played by screen giants like Katharine Hepburn, Tom Hanks, Gene Hackman, Dustin Hoffman, Denzel Washington, Robert Duvall, Michelle Pfeiffer, Cher, John Travolta, Robert Redford, Paul Newman, and even Groucho Marx, and multiple times by actors like Gregory Peck, Spencer Tracy, Al Pacino, Richard Gere, Jimmy Stewart, Harrison Ford, and Tom Cruise (if you include his work in *A Few Good Men*'s military tribunal), clients are often played by the likes of Karate Kid Ralph Macchio in the case of *My Cousin Vinny* or Dick York, the actor probably best known as one of the two men to play Samantha's husband on television's *Bewitched,* in the case of *Inherit the Wind*. Many people know that the name of the lawyer in *To Kill a Mockingbird* is Atticus Finch, and many more know that he was played by Gregory Peck, but expect to be in the upper tiers of *Who Wants to Be a Millionaire?* before being asked the name of the client in that film (Tom Robinson) and who played him (Brock Peters). Even in the film called *The Client*, where one would expect the client to final get his notoriety, it is above-the-title names like Susan Sarandon and Tommy Lee Jones who get to duke it out as the lawyers. A mostly unknown, though very talented, young actor named Brad Renfro gets the title role as client Mark Sway, though admittedly—and deservedly—he does get the largest chunk of screen time.

Of course, there are exceptions in which the client takes center stage as well as top billing, with A-list actors securing the lion's share of movie minutes in the client role. Sean Penn was nominated for the Academy Award for best actor in a leading (not merely supporting) role in *I Am Sam* as the mentally disabled title character who hires lawyer Michelle Pfeiffer to help him keep custody of his daughter. Likewise, Denzel Washington received a similarly well deserved nomination for his leading role as the wrongly convicted boxer in *The Hurricane*. Henry Fonda was also a title character who spends time in the courtroom, but as *The Wrong Man*. James Woods was nominated for an Oscar (albeit in a supporting role) for his performance as the real-life defendant Klansman Byron "Delay" De La Beckwith in *Ghosts of Mississippi*. Robert De Niro chewed up the scenery as Max Cady, a client of costar Nick Nolte, in Martin Scorsese's 1991 remake of *Cape Fear*. De Niro was a client again, this time as real-life gangster Al Capone, for the last scenes of *The Untouchables*. Al Pacino plays at least a former client as the title character in *Carlito's Way*. Don Johnson may have been past his *Miami Vice* prime, but he was still enough of a star to share top billing with Rebecca De Mornay when he played client to her lawyer in *Guilty as Sin*. Kevin Bacon shared top billing with Christian Slater, the actor playing his lawyer, as the defendant who helps shut down Alcatraz with his accusations of prison abuse in *Murder in the First*, and client Jeff Bridges shared top billing with lawyer Glenn Close in *Jagged Edge*.

Both Dustin Hoffman and Meryl Streep were title character clients in *Kramer vs. Kramer*, with the two going head-to-head for custody of their son, though they only become clients per se well into the film. Likewise, Sally Field and Robin Williams battle it out over custody of their children after the title character in *Mrs. Doubtfire* is revealed to be the divorced father, in disguise, simply trying to spend more time with his kids.

Not to be outdone by the men, a number of women superstars have played clients with prominent roles. The murdering divas of *Chicago*, Catherine Zeta-Jones and Renée Zellweger, were both nominated for Oscars (Zeta-Jones won for her supporting role as Velma Kelly, and Zellweger was nominated as a lead actress as Roxie Hart). Zeta-Jones also shared top billing, again as a client, in the Coen brothers' *Intolerable Cruelty*—this time with George Clooney as her attorney. Jodie Foster was nominated for a Best Leading Actress Academy Award for her title role in *Nell*, the final scene of which puts her in a courtroom where her mental competence is being argued. Barbra Streisand was also at the center of a competency hearing when she played the cantankerous Claudia in *Nuts*.

Sometimes the client role, though clearly secondary to the lawyers in the film, is still prominent. In some of these cases, the client role is also be played by a prominent actor. For example, Daryl Hannah played the quirky client in *Legal Eagles*, opposite lawyers Robert Redford and Debra Winger. Samuel L. Jackson was the client defended by lawyer Matthew McConaughey in *A Time to Kill*. Sir Richard Attenborough, more renowned as a director (an Academy Award winner, in fact, for *Ghandi*) than as an actor, was nonetheless familiar to audiences for his work as the inventor of *Jurassic Park* before taking on the client role of Kris Kringle for the 1994 remake of *Miracle on 34th Street*.

Interestingly, these significant but supporting client roles often seem to be the springboard for actors who will later become well-respected leading actors themselves. Much screen time is spent on the client in *Primal Fear*, a good deal of it even out of the presence of the film's star, Richard Gere. The actor playing young Aaron was largely unknown at the time but not so any more—it was Edward Norton, whose Oscar-nominated supporting role in that movie began a now-renowned career that includes films like *Fight Club*. Similarly, a pre-*Schindler* Liam Neeson was far less well known and respected when he played Cher's homeless mute client in *Suspect*.

Tommy Lee Jones, ten years after playing Loretta Lynn's husband in *Coal Miner's Daughter*, had his film career kick started in earnest with his role as the accused conspirator on trial for the John Kennedy assassination in *JFK*. That Oscar-nominated client performance would lead to more roles for Jones, including his Oscar-winning performance in *The Fugitive*, as one of the *Men in Black* in two of those franchise moves, and his turn as Batman villain (and lawyer) Two-Face (aka Harvey Dent) in *Batman Forever*.

This trend of newcomer actors earning their stripes playing clients is not an exclusively modern phenomenon. Although Edmund Gwenn had already appeared in dozens of films over the course of a long movie career, he received his most notoriety when he became the only actor to win an Oscar for playing Santa Claus while portraying him as a client in the original 1947 *Miracle on 34th Street*. That role would lead to his next Oscar nomination three years later in *Mister 880*. Ben Gazzara's film career has spanned close to half a century, and his second screen role (the first to really get any attention) was as the client charged for murdering the man who raped his wife in Otto Preminger's *Anatomy of a Murder*. Judy Holliday played Doris Attinger, the client on trial for murder, in *Adam's Rib*. That small but acclaimed breakthrough role would lead to her Best Actress Academy Award six years later for her portrayal of Billie Dawn in *Born Yesterday*. Holliday's noteworthy career could, in fact, have been legendary if not for the McCarthy communist hearings that harmed all whom they touched, including Holliday.

It would probably be unfair to place Jeremy Irons in the category of an "unknown" when he won a leading actor Oscar for his portrayal of client Claus von Bülow in *Reversal of Fortune*, as he had already received a good deal of acclaim and notoriety for his dual role as the disturbed twin gynecologists in David Cronenberg's *Dead Ringers*, but like the other actors discussed above, it was his client role that really put him on the map and that lead to roles such as Scar in *The Lion King* and Simon Gruber in *Die Hard with a Vengeance*. Unlike the vast majority of these roles, where the client is secondary in prominence to the lawyer or other characters in the film, Wesley Snipes in *New Jack City* played a client who vastly overshadows the lawyers, seen only briefly, even though he admittedly only becomes a client for the last few minutes of the movie.

Although Snipes was not an unknown presence to audiences when he appeared in *New Jack* (he was in Spike Lee's *Mo' Better Blues*), the role of drug kingpin and modern gangster Nino Brown would rocket him into the star category. The film would gain him wide exposure with a more mainstream audience and allow him to secure starring roles in films such as *Rising Sun*, *Demolition Man*, and the *Blade* movies.

Another category of prominent client parts is the lawyer as client. In these films, the lawyer finds himself the subject of a legal proceeding as a client, leading him to ask, as a colleague of Harrison Ford's character in *Presumed Innocent* does, "How does it feel to be on the other side?" In that film, Ford's Rusty Sabich makes the transition from lawyer to client when, as chief deputy prosecutor, he is accused of the murder of a beautiful, ambitious colleague with whom he was having an affair. In *Philadelphia*, Tom Hanks's Andrew Beckett character similarly goes from being a lawyer at a top law firm to a plaintiff when he sues his former employer for discrimination. These films, however, can hardly be used as strong examples of films that go against the rule of clients being almost always upstaged by their lawyers in legal cinema. Because the characters in these films function as both clients and lawyers, it is impossible to speculate how conspicuous they would have been if they were a lawyer or client alone. In fact, this double-threat status might have been a contributing factor that allowed the prominent lawyer/client role to be played by such high-profile actors: Hanks, probably the most Oscar-winning actor of modern times, and Ford, who has been named by motion picture distributors as the most profitable box office star in the history of pictures (think the *Star Wars* and *Indian Jones* trilogies alone).

There is also at least one case in which the judge also acts as the client: John Forsythe as the malevolent Judge Fleming in *. . . And Justice for All*, who is accused of raping and brutally beating a young woman. Even here, however, the judge client is a supporting character—one of many judges in the movie and far secondary to the lawyers, especially Arthur Kirkland, played by the film's star, Al Pacino.

Thus, although there are some notable exceptions, it can be safely characterized as a rule in legal cinema that clients are supporting secondary characters to other legal roles in film, most notably the lawyer. Somehow the client is just not viewed as sufficiently important to warrant the lion's share of attention from spectators of both real-life trials and the trials portrayed in legal cinema.

This subordinate role for clients in film, however, should not be confused with their being inconsequential. On the contrary, the client is often the primary dramatic device used by the writer and director to gain the attention, sympathy, or passion of the audience. Viewers may be unable to remember the client's name or the actor who plays the part, but they will almost always remember the pitiful plight or grave injustice suffered by the client in the film. The audience members may be entranced by the lawyer, but their emotions are more likely to be stirred by the client, whether by the baleful look of a bald, young cancer victim in *Erin Brockovich* or the righteous anger of the father whose ten-year old daughter is beaten, strung up, and raped by redneck, racist thugs in *A Time to Kill*. It is often the client—even one with an insignificant role in the plot—who creates the film's dramatic tension and gives it whatever gravitas it will ever hope to have.

It is probably for this reason that legal cinema has another rule with only a few exceptions: the client is usually innocent and almost always a victim, the more vulnerable and blameless the better. This phenomenon of the almost exclusively innocent client should frankly not come as surprise. How many people would enthusiastically shell out ten dollars to see a lawyer defend some guilty defendant for two hours? Where is the entertainment in that? For most moviegoers, this would simply be taking the concept of the antihero way too far.

The most common type of innocent client in legal cinema is the victim of some corporate or medical wrongdoing that has left the client injured, permanently disabled, or perhaps even clinging to life. In some cases, the actual victim is not the client but must be represented by his or her survivor with the most tragic example being the surviving parent of a dead child.

The entire town of Woburn, Massachusetts, for example, is the plaintiff in *A Civil Action*. Its residents have had their water supply tainted by corporate giants W. R. Grace and Beatrice Foods. As a result, many of the clients are parents of children who suffer with, and in many cases have died of, leukemia. One father tells the heartbreaking story of how he lost his son on the way to the clinic after doctors told him to just wait over the weekend and to bring the boy in on Monday. James Gandolfini plays a plant manager with eight kids, including a son who suffers from seizures and a daughter who has had two miscarriages. His family's plight pushes him to testify against his employer, even at the risk of losing his job. This film, based on an actual case, portrays the clients as both victimized and noble, as when at the outset of the case they tell lawyer Jan Schlictmann, played by John Travolta, that they are "not interested in money." Instead, they say, "What we want is to know what happened. And we want an apology."

Similarly, in *Erin Brockovich*, what starts out as a list of 11 clients becomes a group of 634 plaintiffs—enough to classify the case as *The People of Hinkley, CA v. Pacific Gas and Electric* in another true-life David-and-Goliath battle of sick women and children versus a heartless corporation. The first couple we meet is Donna and Pete Jensen, who do not want to believe that PG&E is responsible for the chromium exposure that has poisoned their family. Later in the film we see Erin trying to comfort her client when Donna finds out she is going to lose her uterus and breasts to the cancer, causing Donna to beg Erin through her tears, "We're gonna get them, aren't we? You gotta promise me we're gonna get them!" We also meet Tom Robinson (presumably no relation to the client with the same name in *To Kill a Mockingbird* but perhaps an homage to him) and his wife, Mandy, who has suffered five miscarriages but blames herself rather than the chromium. Broadway veteran Cherry Jones plays Pam Duncan, who tells of how she brought her kids to the hospital with towels soaked in blood from their nosebleeds only to be accused by county services of abusing them. All of this suffering allows for one of the dramatic highlights of the film, and probably the movie's most memorable moment, when Erin stands up for her clients and confronts the utility company's lawyers, saying, "So before you come back here with another lame-ass offer, I want you to think real hard about what your spine is worth, Mr. Walker. Or what you might expect someone to pay for your uterus, Ms. Sanchez."

The case at the center of *Class Action* is a fictionalized product liability case with similarities to the real-life suit against Ford Motor

Company, the manufacturers of the Pinto, which had a tendency to explode when hit from behind. The class action clients represented by Gene Hackman's Jedediah Tucker Ward include a driver who has survived his accident with only one arm and visible burn scars. We see another client, wheelchair bound, break down during a deposition when shown pictures of the corpses of his dead wife and child, who were in the car that exploded when he was driving. On the other side of the case is the evil car manufacturer, personified in executive George Getchell, played by folksy Fred Thompson. In the movie's "aha" moment, he cooly describes how the company's "bean counters" decide whether to do a recall of a faulty product by comparing the cost of fixing the problem with the cost of letting people get harmed or killed and settling the lawsuits they know will result. At some screenings, you could hear the audience audibly gasp.

Another grieving parent taking on a corporate titan is the catalyst for a movie about jury consultants. In *Runaway Jury*, the mother of a six-year-old gun accident victim and her lawyer are suing the manufacturer of the gun that killed her child. Here the evil gun industry is personified in a CEO with the nefarious, Dickinsonian name Henry Jankle.

The Rainmaker features both a sympathetic victim of a greedy and crooked insurance company and then his grieving mother, who must carry on in his name after his death. The Great Benefits Insurance Company has denied the claim of Donny Ray Black, the young man dying of leukemia, and his family, as it does routinely for each and every claim it receives from its policy holders, telling his mother after the eighth rejection in company correspondence, "You must be stupid, stupid, stupid!" Donny Ray is bleeding from the nose as he signs the retainer contract, marking the document with his dripping blood. In this way the contract is literally a blood pact. The dying client only wants money from his case so his parents will be taken care of after he is gone. Further sympathy is created in that his family is poor; his father is an alcoholic, mentally unstable Vietnam vet with a plate in his head from the war; and the young man is unable to walk without assistance by the time his deposition is taken. His mother, who survives him, is equally sympathetic and selfless, testifying that she will donate every cent of any award they receive to the American Leukemia Society. "Every cent. I don't want a dime of your stinking money," she tearfully tells the insurance company from the witness stand during trial.

Medical malpractice and its victim take center stage in *The Verdict*. Paul Newman, as a down-on-his-luck attorney, brings a suit on behalf of a woman, Sally Doneghy, played by Roxanne Hart, whose sister lies in a coma and whose baby died as the result of being given the wrong anesthetic during delivery. Sally is not suing for monetary gain for herself but for the perpetual care of her sister while she follows her husband to his new job out west. The plight and frustration of many victim clients taking on powerful defendants (in this case, the Archdiocese of Boston) is expressed by the working-class husband, who berates Newman's Frank Galvin for not taking a settlement or even communicating the offer to the clients: "You guys are all the same. . . . It's always what I'm gonna do for you. And then you screw up. . . . And people like us live with your mistakes the rest of our lives."

The victimized client in *Regarding Henry* is not used to create sympathy for the title character lawyer, played by Harrison Ford, but to point out early on how morally bankrupt he is. Before Henry undergoes a metamorphosis from an evil lawyer to the loveable survivor of a bullet to the head, he is in the business of "defending" big hospitals and doctors. In the film's first scene, we see him defending his client from Mr. Matthews, a wheelchair-bound plaintiff, and his elderly, distraught wife. Much later in the film, Henry goes to their apartment to apologize and turn over the witness statement withheld by him and the hospital that would have corroborated the plaintiff's story, saying in his simple way that "What we did was wrong," and "I can't be a lawyer anymore."

In addition to the little-guy client as corporate victim, films often portray clients as being marginalized or from oppressed populations to garner the audience's sympathy. These are people who enter the justice system and its supposedly level playing field already disadvantaged in the larger society. In this way, they are the underdogs even before the trial begins and are suspect even before becoming suspects. This marginalized status they hold in society at large is only compounded by the question of whether anyone in a court of law will believe them, particularly if they are accused of a crime. It also increases the sympathy the audience is likely to feel toward the lowly victim of societal prejudice who now faces the daunting prospect of a trial.

The client in *Suspect*, for example, is both homeless and disabled, someone literally handicapped even before entering the criminal justice system. Carl Wayne Anderson, played by Liam Neeson, is a deaf mute living on the streets, already shunned by society, when he is wrongly accused of murdering a woman. Even his lawyer (played by Cher) refers to him as "The American Nightmare." The more we learn about him, however, the more sympathetic a figure he becomes. We find out he is a Vietnam veteran who had a mental breakdown as the result of his having to kill during the war. His deafness resulted from contracting spinal meningitis in the VA hospital. He confesses his loneliness on the streets when his lawyer asks him whether he can sign, and he writes in response, "No one to talk to." In a symbolic representation of his innocent-victim status, he tells her that he wanted to be a carpenter. This insight, along with his initial appearance in long hair and a beard, conjure up Christ-like comparisons, making him a splendid device to illicit audience sympathy. This positive feeling for the client is only increased by the guilt the audience is likely to feel over the repulsion, or at least skepticism, they felt for the homeless character when he first appeared in the film.

Disability—this time mental disability—is even more central to the plot of *I Am Sam*. The title character, Sam Dawson, played to deserved critical acclaim by Sean Penn, has the intellectual capacity of a seven year old but still tries to be a single father to his daughter, Lucy, after the two of them are abandoned at a bus stop by the girl's mother. Sam is shown to be likeable and of high moral character from the first shot of the film. The credit sequence shows Sam's high work ethic as he meticulously and thoroughly sorts sugar packets at his job as a table cleaner at Starbucks. He is friendly and liked by customers and management. We also see him work valiantly and lovingly to raise his daughter on his own, even taking her to work strapped to his chest. Above all, Sam is shown to be truthful to a fault—even in situations when it disadvantages him. When he is asked whether he can grasp the concept of manipulating the truth, he answers flatly and simply, "No." He even scolds the video image of his daughter when she lies to protect him in a legal proceeding that might result in his losing custody of her. The degree of sympathy created for Sam is vital if the audience is going to overlook the pitfalls of his trying to be a strong father to the girl. We do get scenes of her having to sometimes raise herself, as when she tells her father, "Daddy, tomorrow is my first day of school and I don't want to be sleepy," or when she intentionally plays dumb when her reading level surpasses her father because, as she explains, "I don't want to read it if you can't." But the love of Sam for his daughter and his unwavering honesty and upstanding moral fiber have been so spotlighted in the film that there is no choice but to root for him and his lawyer as they fight for him to remain the custodial parent of the girl, even over the loving foster mom, played by the very likeable Laura Dern.

Jodie Foster's title character in *Nell* turns out in the end to not necessary be mentally disabled, but she is misdiagnosed early on in the film as "severely retarded" by two doctors, played by Liam Neeson and Natasha Richardson. Nell is discovered after her mother dies in the isolated cabin in the woods they shared with Nell's identical twin sister, who died when they were small girls. Because her mother spoke what amounted to her own language, as the result of a series of strokes, Nell was unintelligible and thought to be a mentally disabled "wild child," raised in the wild without any contact whatsoever with the outside world. She becomes a subject for the courts when the doctor, played by Richardson, petitions for and receives a commitment order for Nell, and the doctor played by Neeson fights it with a court order requiring Nell's informed consent before she can be removed from her secluded cabin home. The court orders the two to observe and assess Nell to better inform the court, and they eventually learn her language. The climatic scene in the film is the two doctors fighting in court against Richardson's hospital, which wants to keep Nell as a kind of scientific curiosity. When Nell rises and attempts to address the court directly, the judge must rely on Neeson to interpret her speech. Eventually Nell is released back to her home, and the audience is treated to a happy ending five years later when the now-married doctors visit Nell with their daughter for an annual birthday dinner on a long picnic table outside her cabin. Although Nell has only a perceived disability for the majority of the film, it nonetheless serves the purpose of helping to create the abundant sympathy for this character on which the film depends. Add the death of her mother, the unresolved pain from the childhood death of her twin sister, and the fact that there are reporters, doctors, and ignorant, rough boys from town who are all looking to take advantage of Nell's innocence and vulnerability, and you have one sympathetic character.

The immigrant status or foreign ethic background of a client can also be used to create sympathy for a class of person often held in suspicion by society. One of the accused "six merry murderesses of the Cook County Jail" who performs the "Cell Block Tango" in *Chicago* is an immigrant who does not even speak English. She also appears by her frightened and dazed demeanor to be the only one who actually did not commit the murder of which she is accused. At the very least she is the only woman of the six who does not show glee at the death of her husband. Unfortunately, she is also the first to get the electric chair. Here the victim status of the accused is not used to create dramatic tension or to get the audience dramatically involved in a case but to inject a degree of sobriety to the circus-like atmosphere in which murderers are more concerned with their celebrity status than with acquittals. She provides a reminder of the high stakes involved and some real shame for the lawyers, clients, and others who are manipulating the legal system for their own purposes.

In contrast, the immigrant status of a one-armed burn victim with poor English in *Class Action* is used for the more traditional purpose of getting the audience's sympathy on the side of the lawyer fighting for good and putting the unfeeling corporate client in the most unfavorable light. In *Music Box,* Armin Mueller-Stahl is Mike "Miska" Laszlo, a Hungarian immigrant accused of Nazi war crimes. His immigrant status helps create sympathy for him and add to the belief that his lawyer daughter, played by Jessica Lange, is right to fight to clear him of the accusations. The client in *Twelve Angry Men,* seen only briefly at the beginning but spoken about for the remainder of the film, is not necessarily an immigrant but does appear to be ethnic, perhaps Italian-American. A bigoted juror, played by Ed Begley, constantly refers to him as one of "them."

Clearly the client is young, poor, and scared, sitting silent and on the verge of tears as the jury retires to deliberate. As the deliberations go on, we find out he is only eighteen years old, his mother died when he was nine, and he spent a year and a half in an orphanage while his father was in jail on a forgery charge. He has been arrested multiple times, but he has also been regularly beaten by his father since the age of five. As the white knight Juror #8, Henry Fonda puts it succinctly: "This kid has been kicked around all of his life." His out-of-the-norm ethnic background only helps add to the sympathy that is visually established before the jurors even begin to discuss the case.

In modern times, the homosexual orientation of a client can also be used to create sympathy for the client and his cause. The best example is the portrayal of the gay attorney-turned-client Andrew Beckett in *Philadelphia*. Screenwriter Ron Nyswaner and director Jonathan Demme make sure to overcome any lingering audience bigotry toward their gay main character by also having him contract AIDS and then by showing him rapidly deteriorate throughout the film. The sympathy begins in earnest when we see a sickly Andy leaving the office of the man who will eventually become his lawyer, Joe Miller, played by Denzel Washington. When Andy reaches the street after being rejected for representation by over a half-dozen lawyers, we see the former up-and-comer reduced to a sick, lonely, scared man with lesions and thinning hair who cannot even pay someone to be on his side. In this turning point, he is held in a long close-up, with the mournful sounds of Bruce Springsteen singing the film's title track underneath as Andy is slowly reduced to tears. Later, we see a librarian attempt to move him or, more accurately, quarantine him into a private research room at the library. The whole incident, witnessed by Denzel's character, moves the lawyer to begin thinking about taking the case. Andy only gets worse throughout the film—getting sicker, experiencing great pain and dementia, collapsing at his trial, and eventually lying in his hospital deathbed, bald and unable to breathe without the assistance of a machine. Even before his death, the client is shown as being eternally patient (even when his boyfriend, Miguel, played by Antonio Banderas, loses his cool), industrious, driven, and a lover of justice. It is hard to imagine even the most hard-bitten homophobe making it through the film without feeling that Andy had been wronged and deserved better, which in the broader societal context was probably the purpose of the whole film in the first place: A kind of gay *Roots*, which allowed the general public to understand more intimately the plight of one of America's minority communities. In this way, the sympathetic and almost saintly client serves the purpose of the filmmakers well.

Surprisingly, a sympathetic portrayal of a transgender client appeared years before *Philadelphia* in *...And Justice for All*. At a time when most portrayals of biological men who present themselves as women were used almost exclusively for comedic purposes, Ralph Agee, a transgender person of color, is used in this film to show how society's oppressed become even more victimized in the justice system. When Ralph is sentenced to prison time because of some shoddy lawyering by a stand-in attorney, the terrified client commits suicide in jail. When the client's real lawyer finds out about the case's mishandling, he flies into a rage and demands of the colleague who has bungled the case, but who still shows little sympathy for the dead victim, "Don't you even care? They're just people!" Director Norman Jewison, and especially screenwriters Valerie Curtin and Barry Levinson of *Good Morning Vietnam* and *Rainman* fame, are ahead of their time when they recognize that even during a period when the gay civil rights movement was in its infancy the audience could feel sympathy for a gender-variant person who gets mixed up in a robbery gone bad.

Using characters from marginalized segments of society is not the only way for a director and writer to create sympathy for the client character. Sometimes it is accomplished by using people who are vulnerable or who have survived some kind of abuse. Similar to the out-of-the-mainstream clients (be they homeless, disabled, gay, or transgendered), the vulnerable and abused characters begin with the audience on their side, or at least pitying them. Again, these characters serve as a shortcut to allow the legal film to create sympathy immediately, and thus get the audience rooting even more passionately for the wronged client from very early on in the story.

Children are, of course, naturally vulnerable—or at least are idealized that way by society—so they make excellent candidates for automatically sympathetic clients. How fitting, then, that the film named for clients—*The Client*—features an eleven-year-old child client, Mark

Sway. He may work hard at being tough and independent and even object to being referred to in trial by the lawyers as, simply, "the child," but he is still very much a child in need of protection—particularly when the mob puts out a hit on him. Eventually Mark admits his fear to his mother-figure lawyer Reggie Love, played by Susan Sarandon. Sympathy and the resulting drama are increased because Mark survived abuse by his father before moving into a trailer park with his brother and poor single mother. As discussed earlier, children are also used to great effect to create audience sympathy for the plaintiffs in legal proceedings against evil corporations in films such as *A Civil Action*, *Class Action*, *Erin Brockovich*, and *Runaway Jury*.

Having a client who has suffered physical or sexual abuse at the hands of someone more powerful or in authority is another way of garnering sympathy for a client in a legal film. Call girl Claudia Draper, portrayed by Barbra Streisand in *Nuts*, is suspected of being mentally incompetent after she murders a john played by Leslie Nielsen. We later find out that she was only protecting herself from his vicious attack after she refused to have sex with him. She thrust into Neilsen's neck a shard of glass from a mirror that broke when he slammed her into it, only doing so as he was strangling her in an apparent attempt to kill her. The terror of Nielsen's attack is only compounded when the audience finds out in one of the film's most dramatic sequences that her stepfather, played in a wonderfully creepy role by Karl Malden, used to pay her to have sex with him from the time she was a young girl until she was sixteen. Eventually Claudia is reduced to sobbing on the witness stand and begging the court to protect her from her stepfather, saying, "Don't let him touch me! Don't let him hurt me anymore." Claudia's status as a survivor of abuse, first as a child by her stepfather and then by a john who has paid her to sleep with him, enables her to overcome her crass, stubborn demeanor and gain the audience's sympathy. In *The Rainmaker*, Claire Danes, as Kelly Riker, is also the victim of abuse by a man—in this case her husband. He has routinely used an aluminum bat to beat her, once perhaps causing her, at the age of eighteen, to miscarry. She is terrified to leave him because of his threats to kill her. She eventually becomes a client when she kills him in self-defense and is arrested for manslaughter, but not before establishing herself as a sympathetic survivor of severe domestic abuse.

The client at the center of *Primal Fear* is a victim of sexual abuse, this time by a priest. The defendant, Aaron Stampler (Edward Norton in his breakthrough Academy Award–nominated role), is literally a choirboy and an altar boy, with a boyish face and a southern drawl. He is also arguably disabled by virtue of his speech impediment: a severe stutter. He was a homeless youth before going to Savior House, probably a home for runaways that is based on the real-life Covenant House, a teen shelter in New York City that also had its share of sexual molestation scandals. While living in the Catholic-run facility, Aaron is made to participate in sex acts for the gratification of the archbishop, who videotapes Aaron with another boy and girl who live at the shelter. Aaron's lawyer describes him as looking "like a boy scout." "The victim in this case is my client," the attorney says. "We have two victims and no suspects." Just as the lawyer benefits from making Aaron look like a victim to play on the jury's sympathy, so too do the filmmakers achieve their goals by creating sympathy for this character. These feelings make it all the easier for the writers and director to spring the movie's surprise ending on the audience: This seemingly vulnerable, abused youth is actually a calculating, vicious, manipulative killer. Although the abuse-for-sympathy technique is used for an ulterior motive in this film—to trick the audience rather than get it to simply root for the client and lawyer—it is still an effective way of manipulating the audience for a desired dramatic effect.

A different kind of abuse, but one that still allows a person in authority to abuse his or her position, was the subject of *Murder in the First*. In this film, inspired by a true story, inmate Henri Young is put in solitary confinement for over three straight years after attempting to escape from the infamous Alcatraz prison. Our first view of Henri, and in fact the first shot of the movie, is of a huge steel door slowly swinging open to reveal him lying naked and bloody, crouched in a fetal position, with water being thrown on him. Moments later we see him strung up and being beaten by the sadistic associate warden, played malevolently by Gary Oldman. The prison abuse Young suffers is so horrific that he gets angry when it appears that his lawyer will be successful in getting his sentenced reduced from death to life in prison. "I'd rather die than go back there!" he screams. In fact, he sees death as kind of a welcome relief: "I want to stop being afraid," he explains. In case the audience should attempt to discount its sympathy by recalling that Henri is a convict who did wrong to end up in Alcatraz in the first place, the film explains that the only crime he committed before attempting escape from the prison was to steal five dollars from the cash register of a store that doubled as a post office, making him guilty of the federal crime of mail robbery. He was a juvenile at the time, trying to support himself and his younger sister, who were both orphaned when Henri was ten. Henri even ends the film as a victim when we find out that he is killed in his cell at Alcatraz after his trial, during which the jury admonishes the prison operators for the abuse that had been inflicted on him. The abuse in this film not only serves the purpose of creating necessary sympathy for the convict client but is for all intents and purposes the subject of the film itself—a sort of after-the-fact exposé of the overly harsh conditions that led to the closing of Alcatraz as a federal prison.

In the classic *Adam's Rib*, the abused status of the client is important to lighten the effect of her attempted murder of her adulterous husband and to allow the film to achieve its comic tone. Judy Holliday's Doris Attinger is a poor mother of three and a loyal wife who knows the exact number of days she has been married to her two-timing husband. The hapless housewife is so meek that she needs to read an instruction manual to find out how to fire a gun at her husband when she tracks him into the arms of another woman, played by screen legend Jean Hagen of *Singing in the Rain* fame. Doris gains our sympathy when we find out that her husband is not only a philanderer but also an abusive spouse who has previously beaten her to the point of breaking her teeth. This victimization of the attempted murderess not only sets in motion the story of lawyer Katharine Hepburn decrying the double standard of men being less condemned for adultery than women but it also makes Doris's admittedly criminal action more understandable—even palatable—and thus prevents Hepburn from looking unreasonable for rushing to her defense.

Perhaps the most blatant attempt to make the client a complete target for audience sympathies was when a literal saint—Saint Nick—is put on the stand to determine his sanity in the original and remake versions of *Miracle on 34th Street*. Talk about a sympathetic client! What lawyer would not like the chance to have a client as universally loved as Santa Claus? As Judge Harper's political advisor (played by William Frawley in the original *Miracle*) observes, "You're a regular Pontius Pilate the minute you start!" This Santa is particularly admirable, bringing a love of children, a contempt for commercialism, and a respect for the magic of Christmas into the cynical modern age—whether that age be the mid- or late twentieth century. He confounds his department store employer by sending customers to other stores for less expensive or better-quality gifts, caring only about the happiness of the children. He is motivated to fill in for a drunken Santa at the Thanksgiving Day parade by reminding himself, "The children mustn't be disappointed." In the more modern version, he describes himself by saying, "I'm a symbol of the human ability to be able to suppress the selfish and hateful tendencies that rule the major part of our lives." This is simply a client (and character) who cannot help but be loved. As a result, the cinematic trial (at least in the original version) is one of the most captivating and moving trials ever put on film.

Sometimes the audience is made to feel for the client not because he or she is the injured David against an unfeeling corporate Goliath, because he or she is the member of a marginalized population, or because he or she has been the victim of abuse. Oftentimes, the most compelling client is the one who has been wronged—the client as a victim of injustice. Many of the films involving vulnerable innocents also involve injustice, compounding the audience's sympathies for the client. *Philadelphia* involves a capable, likeable client who had suffered the injustice of losing his job and the esteem of his professional colleagues for no reason other than homophobia and paranoia about AIDS. The plaintiffs in *Erin Brockovich*, *A Civil Action*, and *Class Action* are all victims of corporate greed who had done absolutely no wrong but had their lives and the lives of their families imperiled because companies cut corners or were uncaring about the harm their products or practices inflicted on employees, customers, or neighbors.

Because of the shameful history of slavery in America and the collective White guilt it has engendered, racial injustice can be a powerful way of creating sympathy for a client character. Racial prejudice helps create the dramatic tension for what is arguably the greatest legal film of all time: *To Kill a Mockingbird*. Although the audience is never actually shown the events that lead to the indictment of the "negro" defendant Tom Robinson, it can surmise from the courtroom proceedings that he never beat or raped the young woman who accuses him of the crime. Quite the contrary, she was sexually attracted to Tom and tried to seduce him. When the two of them are discovered by her father, the father beats the girl and either she or two of them together concoct the story of Tom's guilt to clear their own consciences of her daring to pursue a Black man. Tom appears incapable of being violent, particularly toward a White female. He is soft spoken and completely deferential, answering every question on the stand with "yessir" and "no sir." Though he has done nothing wrong, he even appears remorseful as he cries through his testimony on the stand. Perhaps it is fear or righteous anger that moves him to tears. Whatever the motivation, Tom's gentle demeanor together with the glaringly apparent injustice that is being done to him simply because of his race create a dramatic tension in the courtroom scenes that can only be described as electric. The fact that the legal aspect of the film is really only a fraction of a story that involves the love of family members for each other, the burdens of being a man of principle, and the loss of childhood innocence only speaks to the film's richness and greatness.

Racial injustice is also a factor used to justify a father's murder of the attackers who beat and raped his daughter in *A Time to Kill*. The two White attackers in *A Time to Kill* are unapologetic racists who torment and antagonize Black citizens in their rural Mississippi town before kidnapping and savagely raping the 10-year-old daughter of Carl Lee Hailey, played by Samuel L. Jackson. Much of the audience might have been predisposed to applaud the vigilante justice dispensed by the father, who shot the men as they entered the courthouse to be tried for their crimes. For those who would say he should have waited for the justice system to take its course, novelist John Grisham and screenwriter Akiva Goldsman use racial dynamics to bring the audience more passionately to Carl Lee's side. As Carl Lee himself explains to his lawyer, "How is a Black man ever going to get a fair trial with the enemy on the bench, in the jury box, my life in White hands?" Further sympathy is created for Carl Lee when he sneaks to the hospital to see the police officer he unintentionally maimed during the attack, in order to take responsibility and apologize. He is also shown to be loyal, sticking by his attorney even when the National Association for the Advancement of Colored People comes to town to strong-arm him into letting them defend him with their handpicked lawyers. However, more than the admirable personality traits of the defendant, the lion's share of sympathy for the client is created by the question hovering over the entire proceedings of whether a Black man who killed two White men could ever get a fair trial in the Deep South.

The real-life defendant Rubin "Hurricane" Carter also makes for such a sympathetic client character in *The Hurricane* because he is a victim of racial injustice. Rubin is an innocent man, but as he says in the film, "Innocence is a highly overrated commodity.... I've committed no crime. The crime has been committed against me." He is framed for murder by a corrupt, racist police sergeant who withholds evidence and strong-arms witnesses, including two parolees whom he threatens with jail time unless they change their story and identify Rubin as the culprit in the barroom shooting of four unarmed victims. Despite being a cause célèbre for prominent figures including Muhammad Ali and Bob Dillon, Hurricane ends up serving decades in prison before being cleared and set free. He recognizes that racism has cheated him of most of his life when he tells a fellow inmate, "Everything I lost that really matters, I lost at the hands of White folks." Yet the film portrays Carter nobly as having little ill will for the White race as a whole. On the contrary, Rubin says of the young Black man and his three White guardians who work tirelessly to free him, "Hate put me in prison. Love is gonna bust me out."

Portrayals in legal cinema of racial injustice against innocent clients are not limited to African American defendants. Yuji Okumoto plays Korean-American Shu Kai Kim in *True Believer*. He has spent eight years in prison for a murder he did not commit, but for which he was framed by an ambitious prosecutor. At one point Kim's lawyer, Eddie Dodd, played by James Woods, confronts the district attorney, played by Kurtwood Smith. He says to the district attorney, who rose to fame cracking a Colombian drug ring, "Colombians, Koreans, what's the difference? You built your career putting non-Whites behind bars, haven't you?"

Closed mindedness of another kind is used to create sympathy for the client on trial in *Inherit the Wind*. Bertram Cates, played by Dick York, is a teacher being prosecuted for breaking the law and daring to teach the theory of evolution to his high school class. He repeatedly tries to convince the world that he is a pawn caught in a struggle between enlightenment and religious faith, saying things like, "I just want to teach," and, "I'm just a school teacher." In fact, however, he is quite righteous in his commitment to knowledge and risks his career and freedom to teach Darwin and his theory. He even chooses his right to teach over his true love, a preacher's daughter, when he refuses to give up the case that is ripping them apart. The film does not hide whose side it is on, creating additional sympathy for the schoolteacher by portraying the townsfolk as ignorant, bible-thumping thugs. The opening shot of the film is of the Hillsboro courthouse sign with the film's theme song, "Gimme That Old Time Religion," being sung underneath. This is as balanced as the film gets in portraying whether there is any legitimacy in the tension that exists in America between religion and the law. Any philosophic existentialism on this question is shattered in the film's next shot, showing a mob of townspeople burning the school teacher in effigy, signing and chanting, "We'll hang Bert Cates from a sour apple tree" as they march past the blindfolded statue of justice. The film clearly portrays Cates as a victim of injustice, fighting for what it characterizes as the proper outcome of reason over ignorance.

Sometimes the clients in legal films are made to be sympathetic not so much because they are victims of callous or even intentional injustice but simply because they are wrongly accused or, as Alfred Hitchcock put it in his classic crime drama, *The Wrong Man*. In that film, based on a true story of mistaken identity, the client, Manny Balestrero, played by the ever-likeable Henry Fonda, is sympathetic not only because he has been wrongly accused, arrested, jailed, and arraigned for crimes he did not commit but also because he is portrayed as a poor, struggling musician working nights to try and provide for his family; a loving husband to his wife (Vera Miles) who is driven to a mental breakdown by his ordeal; a good father to two young boys; a dutiful son to his presumably immigrant Italian mother, an optimist who says to his wife, "I think we're pretty lucky people, mostly;" a temperate man who does not drink even though he works in a nightclub; and a faithful man who prays the rosary in court. Oh, and did we mention that he is Henry Fonda?

The wrong man scenario is also used to create sympathies for clients and, more important, their lawyer—the title character played by Joe Pesci in the superior courtroom comedy *My Cousin Vinny*. When two "youts" (as Vinny memorably calls them in his thick Brooklyn accent) are driving through Beechum County, Alabama, on their way from New York University to the University of California, Los Angeles, as they prepare to transfer schools, they are mistaken for two men who have held up and shot the clerk at the Sac-O-Suds grocery store. These are good kids, innocent and scared, as well as being fish-out-of-water, ethnic city boys: Ralph Macchio plays the Italian-American William Gambini, and Mitchell Whitfield is Stanley Rothenstein, who will have another cinematic run-in with the law as a member of Alan Dershowitz's legal team in *Reversal of Fortune*. By allowing Vinny to fight for innocent clients—one of them a family member—the filmmakers make the lawyer more likable and admirable, allowing the film to be both funny and feel-good when the unorthodox Vinny, ably assisted by his fiancée, played by Marisa Tomei in her Academy Award–winning role, clear the innocent clients of their supposed crimes.

. . . And Justice for All uses a tragically innocent client to point out the insensitivity and ineptitude of the justice system in the 1970s. Arthur Kirkland's client, Jeff McCullaugh (Thomas Waites), has been imprisoned because he has been wrongly identified as a murderer, but the judge hearing the case will not set him free because the evidence proving his innocence was submitted three days late. In prison, he gets beat up and raped, to which his judge (the same one who becomes a client himself when he is accused of rape) says, "Good! Let those criminals create their own hellhole."

This is not to say that all clients portrayed in film, sympathetic though they may be, are likable. Some victimized client characters are quite unpleasant or even downright nasty. The Mark Sway character in *The Client*, for example, is far from a cherubic model child. The first shot of the film is of him stealing two cigarettes from his mother's purse and then running off with them and his brother into woods against her direct orders. He has no compunction about lying to a police officer to cover the fact that he was off smoking with his brother in the woods when they came across a suicide victim. Later on, after he is taken into protective custody, he precociously, cleverly, and dishonestly plays on the sympathy of a prison guard, acting like a scared child to get access to a phone and fraudulently charge dozens of pizzas to the credit card he stole from the detective who arrested him. Finally, he fakes a seizure to get out of jail and back to the hospital, where his brother lies in a comatose state. He is prone to profanity, as when he says, "I don't give a flying shit about the FBI," or when he responds to his lawyer's request that they talk by saying, "Talk, my ass, you're fired!" And he is defiant to the end: As he and his family are being placed in the witness protection program and being told he can never see his lawyer and friend Reggie again, his last words to her are, "I'll call you." But even the negative traits of this tough character seem to be bluster covering his true nature. He is inclined to do the right thing, even at the cost of putting himself in danger, as when he tries to prevent the suicide of mob lawyer Jerome "Romey" Clifford at the beginning of the film. He cannot bring himself to pull the trigger and shoot Romey, even after it appears Romey is going to kill the two of them. Mark is protective of his little brother lying in a coma and attacks a reporter who attempts to take his brother's picture. And he cannot lie to his mother when she asks him directly about what happened out in the woods. In short, he is a streetwise but good boy on the edge of adolescence: moral, rough around the edges, and at times a real pain in the ass.

Likewise, before the title heroine in *Erin Brockovich* started working in a law office, she was a client whom no one would ever confuse as a summa cum laude graduate of the Miss Manners Finishing School. She is a no-nonsense, plain talker who swears a lot, even on the stand as a witness at her own trial in a personal injury case. She is easily excitable and quick to get loud and confrontational. Even after she guilt-trips her former lawyer into hiring her as a secretary/paralegal, she is not exactly an obedient Employee of the Month. When her boss tries to politely and supportively suggest that she rethink her revealing work outfits, she tells him, "You might want to rethink those ties." Still, she is shown as noble, down on her luck, and supremely sympathetic. She is a poor single mom of three, including an infant with a cough. After being rejected for a job, she is struck by a driver running a red light. She sacrifices for her children, passing up dinner at a restaurant with her kids because she cannot really afford the meal. Again, she is an at-times unpleasant client whose rough exterior covers a heart of gold.

Similarly, Barbra Streisand's Claudia character in *Nuts* is difficult, defiant, blunt, and even vulgar. When being interviewed by her lawyer, she asks him, "You have a missus? She give good head?" When the subject of her occupation as call girl comes up when she is on the witness stand, she gives the court a very detailed menu: "I get $400 for a straight lay, $300 for a hand job, $500 for head." She yells at her lawyer after he goes to her apartment to get her clothes for her trial, screaming, "Who said you could go to my apartment? . . . What gives you the right to invade me?" Once again, however, this rough demeanor is balanced with her more admirable or sympathetic qualities, such as when she hugs, dotes on, and "mothers" her mother after reconciling with her, even though her mother seemed to knowingly turn a blind eye to her husband's sexual abuse of Claudia as a girl. She also confesses the fear that underlies her bluster and her pain at having acquiesced to her stepfather's sexual overtures because, "I just wanted him to love me."

Daryl Hannah's character in *Legal Eagles* is not so much rude as flakey, and perhaps manipulative. She is first seen as an angelic child who witnesses the murder of her artist father, thus establishing sympathy for her early on. She becomes a beautiful, sexy performance artist who is not above using sex to charm the district attorney who is prosecuting her, or to get information from her father's former business partner. As an indication of her instability, however, she brings a gun along when she goes to visit the partner and question him about her father's missing paintings. One character questions whether she is "emotionally disturbed." Overall, however, she is portrayed as having severely bad judgement but being a sympathetic victim nonetheless.

A number of clients are also portrayed as having committed a violent act—sometimes shockingly violent—but are able to have the sympathy for the characters maintained by portraying the violence as justified. Both the Doris Attinger client in *Adam's Rib* and the majority of the murdering mistresses on death row in *Chicago* attempted or committed murder only because of the philandering, adulterous activities of their husbands or boyfriends. Lieutenant Frederick "Manny" Manion, played by Ben Gazzara in *Anatomy of a Murder*, is a jealous and suspicious husband, described by his lawyer as, "insolent and hostile. Worst of all, he appears to beat his wife fairly regularly. Still, he is a decorated Korean War veteran." Manion finally becomes a murderer when he shoots the man who raped his wife. Even then, he retains his sympathetic stature because, as explained by his lawyer, "[Y]ou're wife was raped. You'll have a favorable atmosphere in the courtroom. The sympathy will be with you." In *Murder in the First*, Henri Young uses a spoon to the neck to kill the inmate and fellow Alcatraz escapee who falsely ratted him out as the mastermind of the escape plan. Later, he is also shown to be antisocial, when he begins masturbating in front of his new female lawyer while looking up her skirt, but the whole premise of the movie is that it was his mistreatment in Alcatraz, including three years alone in a dark, filthy dungeon cell, that led him to the brink of insanity and to his undesirable behavior. Carl Lee Hailey, in *A Time to Kill*, shoots two men at point-blank range in front of dozen of witnesses. He shows no remorse, but on the contrary, says defiantly, "I'm not sorry for what I done." However, his act of violence is motivated by the blind rage caused by the fact that his two victims raped his 10-year-old daughter.

A whole set of other clients exhibit a violent act when provoked but later show their true, more peaceful nature. Carl Wayne Anderson in *Suspect* assaults his court-appointed attorney shortly after being incarcerated, as does Claudia in *Nuts*. Claudia even goes one better and punches her first lawyer in the middle of the trial before being pulled from the courtroom, grasping at the American flag as she goes. In the original *Miracle on 34th Street*, Kris uses his cane to give a tap to the head of the store psychologist who was working beyond his expertise and performing psychotherapy on another employee, a "young, impressionable" friend of Kris's. In the more modern *Miracle*, Kris's violence is a little more extreme, but so is the provocation: The victim is paid to bait Kris into assaulting him, even accusing him of being a child molester, and then plays it to the hilt when Kris finally does attack him. In all these cases, however, the violence is largely an aberration brought about by an uncharacteristic emotional outburst and thus does little to get in the way of the sympathy that the audience ultimately ends up feeling for the client.

Sometimes, though, the violence rises to the level of vicious or even sadistic, but the client is shown to have been a victim him or herself to some degree nonetheless. Although the clients in *Chicago*, Velma, Roxie, and Lucy Liu's Kitty Baxter, all use deadly force in shooting a man, they were all also used by the men they murdered. Velma's husband cheated on her with her sister, Roxie's victim lied about his showbiz connections to get her to sleep with him, and Kitty committed a triple homicide after catching her husband in bed with two women. In this way, although all three characters are clearly violent murders, there can still be sympathy for them, for as Fred Ebb's lyrics put it, "It was murder but not a crime."

Even crime figures can be shown as sympathetic in legal films. Besides the "Butcher Boy of St. Mike's," Richard Gere's other client in *Primal Fear* is Joey Pinero, a gangster who, we are told, "has done a lot of good for [the] community," such as building a clinic and stopping the neighborhood from being razed for high-rent condos. Eventually he is assassinated by powerful real estate investors.

Client, or at least former client, Carlito Brigante in *Carlito's Way* is shown early in the film claiming to be "born again" and "changed" after being released from prison on a technicality after serving five of his thirty-year sentence. His conversion is shown to be genuine when he lets everyone know that he wants out of his racketeering past. He even takes a legitimate job, working hard as the manager of a nightclub. Unfortunately, events seem to conspire against him. He gets sucked back into his gangster ways when he innocently accompanies his young cousin on a drug run gone bad, and Carlito has to massacre a room full of heavies to defend his cousin and save himself. He is portrayed as a tragic figure in the traditional Greek sense: a victim of destiny and fate. As he puts it, "I didn't invite this shit, it just comes to me. I run, it runs after me. Gotta be somewhere to hide." Further sympathy is created for Carlito when he forgives an old fiend who has worn a wire in an attempt to frame Carlito and subject him to another arrest. More than anything else, Carlito is loyal to a fault, putting himself at risk to help his increasingly out-of-control lawyer, David Kleinfeld. "Kleinfeld is my brother," Carlito says. "He saved my life! . . . I owe him. That's who I am. That's what I am, right or wrong. I can't change that!"

Far more ruthless is Wesley Snipes's Nino Brown in *New Jack City*, who, for all his cruelty, is still shown to be somewhat a victim of his times. The first shot of the movie has Nino looming over a man being hung by his feet and then dropped of a bridge for not paying his debts. Later, Nino takes a cue from Al Capone in *The Untouchables* and knifes one of his lieutenants through the hand after their headquarters is infiltrated. He slays his brother and partner à la *The Godfather.* He uses a little girl to shield himself from gunfire during a mob hit. He even beats a kid to death with a bat, douses him with gasoline, and sets him on fire for shorting him five dollars. Still, director Mario Van Peebles strongly makes the point that greed in corporate America and the nation at large helps create vicious, ruthless characters in the underworld as well. The movie opens with overhead shots of New York, starting with the Statute of Liberty below the financial district and moving uptown to Harlem. On the soundtrack, meanwhile, we hear news reporters giving statistics about income disparity, new high levels of homelessness, rising unemployment, and an increase in drug-related crimes, including the death of a five-year old child. Nino says, "You gotta rob to get rich in the Reagan era." He refers to himself as "the new American dream" and says of his cruelty, used to keep and increase his drug trade, "This is big business. This is the American way." Even on the stand at his trial he explains, "I was dealing drugs ever since I was twelve years old. But I was forced into this way of life." Van Peebles does not attempt to justify Nino's brutality, but he does contextualize the drug kingpin client and prevent the audience form feeling pure contempt for the film's main character.

Even the psychotic Max Cady, played by Robert De Niro in Scorsese's 1991 *Cape Fear*, is shown to be somewhat of a victim—this time of a lawyer who failed his oath to vigorously defend his client. Max's menacing evil is undeniable. He tells his former lawyer, Sam Bowden, played by Nick Nolte, "You're gonna learn about loss." He then poisons Bowden's family dog and later savagely attacks and rapes Bowden's female friend and coworker. Eventually, Cady tries to rape Bowden's daughter while Cady and his wife are forced to watch. The whole thing gets a little farcical, with Max becoming a sort of evil supervillain capable of riding strapped beneath a car for hundreds of miles, taking a face full of boiling water without flinching, and being set on fire only to rise again out of the swollen river. But for all his cruelty, Max is correct in asserting that he was "betrayed" by his lawyer when Sam withheld information that would have let Cady avoid the guilty verdict on the rape he had committed. In a mock trial he conducts at gunpoint, Max forces Bowden to quote the ethical canons of the American Bar Association—that he will zealously represent his client. "I find you guilty of judging me and selling me out!" Max screams at Sam. "You were my lawyer! You were my lawyer!" he says almost through tears. Sam's decision to act as Max's judge and not his lawyer cost Max fourteen years in prison, where he was raped, as well as the loss of his wife and daughter, who left him after he was incarcerated. Few audience members are likely to cheer Max on as an aggrieved victim, but in this later version of the movie there is depth added to the character from the original *Cape Fear*, where this betrayal aspect was completely missing. (The original Max Cady, played malevolently by Robert Mitchum, is not technically a client, at least not until he retains a lawyer to accuse Sam and the sheriff of harassing him to leave town.) In the updated version of the film, Max is not simply pure evil, but a wronged man who could have been empathetic if he were not so vengeful and cruel.

Catherine Zeta-Jones's portrayal of client Marylin Rexroth in *Intolerable Cruelty* as ruthless and devious serves the purpose of making her turnaround at the film's conclusion all the more romantic. Throughout the film, she is shown preying on husbands for their money. When lawyer Miles Massey, played with aplomb by George Clooney, orders her steak at dinner and says, "I assume you are a carnivore," Marylin laughs seductively and says, "Oh, Mr. Massey, you have no idea," echoing the line from another cinematic client, Jeremy Irons as the steely Claus von Bülow in *Reversal of Fortune*. Marylin fakes being distraught during her divorce trial until she is exposed by Miles as having sought out her rich philandering husband as a patsy. She then vows to "marry again. Nail the guy's ass good." Her scheme to marry and then divorce the lawyer who cost her the riches of her first husband, however, ends when she eventually comes to love Miles for richer and for poorer—and even without a prenuptial agreement. Even in a film called *Intolerable*

Cruelty, the seemingly cruel client can and does come around to being a loving, vulnerable human being.

Similarly, Parker Posey as the client seeking a divorce in *Laws of Attraction* goes from bitter divorcée to romantic. She starts off asking her lawyer, "Can we just skip to the part where you cut his balls off?!" This, however, is just initial anger at her husband's betrayal. Later, the two reconcile and are shown very much in love.

There is no such redemption for the client Benny Gibbs, played by Rip Torn in *Trial and Error*. He has been indicted for fraud after bilking people into paying $17.99 plus shipping and handling for a copper engraving of Abraham Lincoln that turns out to be a penny. It is unclear, however, whether this guilty client is also a victim. He tells an elaborate sob story to the court about a Halloween party fire at the orphanage where he lived as a child that led to an addiction to sweets (don't ask). This becomes sort of a warped "Twinkie defense" for the client. There is strong indication that he is completely lying, but because his testimony on the witness stand is played for comic effect, it blends into the rest of the movie's outlandish attempts at broad comedy. Even if he is a victim, however, Benny comes close to being portrayed as completely unsympathetic. As the man acting as his lawyer (Michael Richards) states, "He's never taken responsibility for anything he's ever done." As a result, this is a movie much less about the trial of a guilty and probably completely reprehensible client and more about peripheral characters dealing with the importance of being true to one's self and of being responsible for the decisions we make in our lives.

The guilty and reprehensible client is used in the exact same way and to a much more effective and entertaining effect in *Liar Liar*. Here Jennifer Tilly plays divorcee Samantha Cole, a shrill, vindictive woman who seemingly dislikes her children but is not above demanding full custody of them just to hurt her husband. She tears them from his arms as she leaves the courtroom saying, "Those are mine. . . . You haven't paid for them yet!" However, as with *Trial and Error*, this film is not about this client. She only serves the purpose of allowing the formerly equally immoral lawyer, played by Jim Carrey, to see the error of his ways and redeem himself through his revelation about how dishonesty has hurt his life. Thus, even in films such as these, in which the clients are purely guilty, the filmmakers attempt to make the experience palatable to the audience by giving the client little screen time and using him or her as living proof of where a life built on lies will lead.

There are a few instances in which filmmakers manage to make a compelling and even entertaining story almost completely about the defense of a purely and irredeemably guilty man—one who has not even been a victim himself to make it easier for the audience to tolerate such an intense focus on the character. The best examples actually prove the rule of the presumption of innocence of the client in legal cinema. The aforementioned *Primal Fear* actually turns the audience's forgone assumption that the client must be innocent against its viewers to allow for its surprise twist ending. The client, Aaron, appears to have a multiple personality disorder that makes him become the ruthless killer "Roy" to exact revenge on the priest who has been sexually abusing him. In the turning point of the movie though, Roy tells us that "there never was an Aaron," and that he has fooled his lawyer, the justice system, and the audience into letting him be found insane, presumably to be let out of prison in weeks. The filmmakers rub salt into our wounds by making Aaron/Roy not only guilty and sneaky but loathsome as well. On murdering his unfaithful girlfriend and Archbishop Rushman, the client tells his lawyer, after getting off, "That cunt just got what she deserved. But cutting up that son-of-a-bitch Rushman, that was just a work of art."

Similarly, *Music Box* keeps the audience guessing throughout the film whether the client is innocent of the barbaric war crimes of which he is accused. The presumption of client innocence is compounded here by sympathy created for the character by showing him taunted by protesters in front of his house who throw rocks through his window and by showing his love for his children and grandchildren. Again, the expectation that the client will be cleared of guilt allows for the film's ultimate revelation to come as a shocking surprise. As in *Primal Fear*, we feel not only duped but betrayed to find out, along with his lawyer, that this kindly old man, played so sympathetically by Armin Mueller-Stahl is, in fact, as characterized by the prosecuting attorney, "evil incarnate." The leader of a Nazi Hungarian death squad, Lazlo is proven by old black-and-white photos hidden inside a music box to be a sadistic killer who gang-raped a sixteen-year-old girl and who enjoyed killing Jews and gypsies by wiring entire families together and shooting a few members in the head before dumping them all into the freezing Danube river.

The film noir–ish *Jagged Edge* also uses at least doubt about the guilt of its accused client as a means of building suspense and providing a surprise ending. The defendant client in this case is Jack Forrester (played by Jeff Bridges), a rich and powerful San Francisco newspaper editor. His wife has been sadistically murdered, and he has been accused of the crime. He is portrayed in the first half of the film as a decent man wrongly accused by an ambitious district attorney. Bridges will not resort to low tactics for his own benefit, telling the reporters at his newspaper, "I don't want any slant, any bias on our coverage of my case or of [the district attorney], do you hear me?" He breaks down, sobbing violently when he first returns to the bedroom where his wife was murdered. We are told the polygraph machine "loves him" and that his line remained totally even when questioned on the murder. Later, however, the seeds of doubt are sown. A psychologist paid to examine him tells his attorney, "He didn't get to where he is without being manipulative." We find out he has been cheating on his wife. One witness testifies, "That was his special talent, he really knew how to use people." His own attorney accuses him by saying, "You played me so well. You set me up from the very beginning." The district attorney, played by Peter Coyote, finally lays it on the line, saying, "He planned this [murder] for eighteen months! He's not a psychopath. He's an iceman. He's a monster!" The ambivalent information, however, together with the presumption that movie clients are innocent, still allows for a final shock plot twist when the defense attorney, played by Glenn Close, finds a hidden typewriter in the home of her client, which he used throughout the trial to feed her information that only the killer would know.

For far lighter purposes, the surprise twist of the client actually being guilty is used in *Wild Things* to change the story from the tale of manipulative high school girls accusing a seemingly innocent client to one of the perfect extortion plot conducted by the accused client and his accomplices. Again, filmmakers pour sympathy on top of the presumption of innocence to show Sam Lombardo, played by Matt Dillon, as an award-winning "Educator of the Year" and a popular guidance counselor accused of rape by a very rich girl, leading him to be ostracized before even going to trial. He is beaten up, run off the road, cut off from his girlfriend, and fired from his job, all because of what appears to be the revenge of a jilted student. After his trial, however, the audience is shocked to find out that he orchestrated the arrest with his accusers. As the movie progresses, we see Sam as a "stone-cold manipulative psychopath," as characterized by the detective, played by Kevin Bacon, and even see him become a murderer, killing off his co-conspirator and lover and then framing his other co-conspirator and lover for the first girl's death. It all amounts to a dark but playful if somewhat implausible hour and a half of fun, all possible because the audience is tricked into believing, as is almost always the case, that the accused client is an innocent victim.

A surprise plot twist can also be achieved by having apparently guilty clients turn out to be innocent. *The Star Chamber* takes great pains (and a great deal of screen time) to do away with any preexisting pro-client bias the audience may have and instead establish the guilt and viciousness of a number of clients. Then, over an hour into the movie, the audience can be surprised when two men accused of running a child pornography ring are later discovered to be innocent. This sets up a crisis of conscience for Judge Steven Hardin, played by Michael Douglas, who has joined a secret society of judges that pronounces its own verdicts and dispenses its own vigilante justice on the guilty. He has instigated a "death sentence" against these two men who were found to be innocent. The other truly guilty and loathsome clients shown earlier in this film are used to create the justification for the film's gimmick: a group of judges who use the law every day but who take it even more firmly into their own hands when they meet secretly at night as part of the Star Chamber (even though at no point in the film is the group actually called that). Even the necessary guilty clients in this film, however, are quickly forgotten after they have served their plot purpose. For example, after the film spends the first act focusing on the trial of a man who has cold-bloodedly killed five elderly women for their welfare checks, the client is never heard from again. He never even makes into in the Star Chamber to be held accountable for his crimes. Even in a film such as *The Star Chamber*, the guilty client is a necessary evil who must be gotten off screen as quickly as is possible.

Presumed Innocent has a title that is largely truth in advertising: The lawyer-client in the film's climatic trial is presumed innocent not only in a legal sense but as all film clients are. But the film has a satisfying double-twist ending in which one minute it appears that Harrison Ford's Rusty Sabich got away with murder, only to find out a minute later that it was his wife who was guilty in killing his mistress. The presumption of innocence of the cinematic client allows for one surprise ending when he appears guilty and then another when the apparently guilty client is shown as innocent.

There is at least one film, however, without any surprise twist and in which the client who is the star of the film is without any redeeming qualities whatsoever and without any history of victimization that might lead to at least some air of audience sympathy. *Guilty as Sin* tells the client-as-stalker story of David Greenhill, a handsome gigolo played by Don Johnson who is accused of throwing his most recent wife out of their apartment window. "I've lived off women my whole life," he arrogantly tells his lawyer. "It's all I'm good at. It's my talent. Getting women to do what I want them to do." He is also a self-described compulsive womanizer. Even his own lawyer points out, "You don't portray yourself as a very sympathetic figure." That, unfortunately, is putting it mildly. The audience comes to find that he has murdered many women and that his lawyer is his latest object of obsession. He works to destroy her relationship with her fiancée and eventually savagely attacks the other man with a pipe. Greenhill is revealed to be a cold-blooded, vile monster. He explains that he took his gloves off to murder his wife because, "It felt better. . . . Killing with gloves would be like fucking with a rubber." This movie is perhaps the only one in the complete history of legal cinema to have a 100 percent irredeemable, reprehensible, and loathsome main character client. That, in fact, seems to be the whole point: To create a thriller with a new twist, the client who manipulatively victimizes his lawyer. Perhaps the deservedly lackluster reception that greeted the film both critically and at the box office indicates why the rule against unlikable clients is so rarely broken in Hollywood.

In some films, the filmmakers make the unsympathetic client more palatable by diminishing the client role and almost disguising the victim as the true client. This technique is particularly easy to achieve in films involving criminal trials that focus on the district attorney, or the crime victim and his or her family. In this way, the victim arguably *is* a client—"The People" represented by the district attorney, as the television show *Law & Order* describes it in its opening narration. This point of view is articulated explicitly by the father in *The Star Chamber* grieving for the kidnapping, sexual torture, and murder of his ten-year-old son when he points out to Michael Douglas's Judge Hardin, "That was my little boy. That's what this [trial] is all about. Nothing else. Nothing else!" Understandably for him, the client of relevance is not the accused but the victim of the crime.

Whoopi Goldberg, playing the widow of civil rights leader Medgar Evers in *Ghosts of Mississippi,* is not technically the client in that film, though the lawyer prosecuting the case, played by Alec Baldwin, treats her as if she were. He calls her regularly with status reports about the case against her husband's murderer. By focusing on the Evers widow and her decades-long struggle to achieve a conviction against the White man who assassinated her husband, director Rob Reiner and writer Lewis Colick are able to sympathetically involve the audience in the trial, even with a hate-spewing racist as the real client.

Similarly, in *The Accused,* it is easy to forget that the clients in the film are the guilty perpetrators of a heinous crime: Encouraging and cheering on the gang rape of a young woman. The viewer is tempted to mistake Jodie Foster's character, Sarah Tobias, as the title character—the accused. This is probably no accident, as the film attempts to highlight what was then the common practice of revictimizing the rape victim by putting her and her sexual practices on trial as part of defending the rapists. It is easy to forget that the film features not one but two trials in which Sarah is not the client.

The abusive mother on trial during part of *Presumed Innocent* is barely seen. Instead, the film shows more of Prosecutor Rusty Sabich with her 5-year-old son, Wendell, who, looking so small and meek on the witness stand, tells the court how "my mommy hurt my head" by putting it in a vice. Again, the victim of the crime is made to appear to be the client of Harrison Ford's chief deputy prosecutor, while the real client—the mother being charged with the crime—does not even get to speak a line in the movie.

Occasionally, the guilty client is also portrayed as loathsome to show the depths to which the lawyer has fallen. In *The Devil's Advocate*, for example, the clients of the ambitious young lawyer Kevin Lomax (Keanu Reeves) range from a child-molesting eighth-grade teacher, who begins covertly masturbating in court as his victim testifies about her molestation, to Trump-like real estate developer Alexander Cullen, played by Craig T. Nelson, who is accused of killing his wife, stepson, and maid, and who is at least guilty of sleeping with his young stepdaughter. Both these despicable clients are used to show how amoral Reeves's Lomax is, and how his interest in winning overrides any conscience about setting guilty people free. Similarly, in *Class Action*, the contemptible corporate clients guilty of knowingly selling faulty cars that can kill their passengers allow the audience to draw comparisons between the righteous crusader Jedediah Tucker Ward, played by Gene Hackman, and his mercenary gun-for-hire daughter, corporate lawyer Maggie Ward, played by Mary Elizabeth Mastrantonio. To allow the makers of both these films to avoid any possibility of alienating the audience with these unsympathetic and guilty clients, the clients' roles are small, and they are kept on the screen just long enough to illustrate the point that the lawyer has sold his or her soul to the devil—literally so in Kevin Lomax's case.

Legal cinema, then, has two well-established precedents. First, keep the client role small or at least secondary to the other characters in the film, especially the lawyers. Second, make the client innocent or at least sympathetic. Filmmakers know these rules well, and although they occasionally deviate from them to trick an audience, they have little interest in trying to break them outright, for filmmakers are not interested in making an appeal to a higher court, but in making their films appeal to their audiences. It appears from an overview of clients in legal cinema that there is nothing quite like an innocent, victimized client hovering in the background to get the audience right where the filmmakers want them: squarely on their side.

2

All Rise: The Judge

"What do you think we are? Umpires, sweetheart. Everyday we get the lineup cards and then explain the ground rules to the managers.... It's always been a game."
—Hal Holbrook as Judge Benjamin Caulfield in *The Star Chamber*

In the American legal system, if the lawyers are the intellectual gladiators, the judge is the referee. "My responsibility is to ensure a fair trial for the accused," Michael Douglas says succinctly as Judge Steven R. Hardin in *The Star Chamber*. At least one cinema judge, Judge Weaver in *Anatomy of a Murder*, even adopts the combat metaphor when he says to the lawyers who are sparring in chambers in a seemingly civil but strategic repartee, "Skirmish over. Shall we join now on the field of battle?" In *Primal Fear*, a lawyer uses the sports metaphor to explain why he did not want to be a judge: "Why become an umpire when you can play ball?" Unlike some other countries, in which a judge or tribunal of judges is involved in questioning witnesses and other parties to the case or has a hand in the investigation phase of a proceeding before a trial even begins, American judges are supposed to be impartial arbitrators, to be almost removed from the specific facts of a case. The judge is so neutral that he or she is not even authorized to address any shortcomings in the fairness of a case unless it is first objected to by one of the attorneys. We see this displayed cinematically in *The Rainmaker*, when a sympathetic judge who clearly sees improper questions being asked by the defendant's lawyers to a witness nonetheless restrains himself from saying a word when the brand-new counsel for the plaintiff does not know when or how to object.

Although the judge will be very involved throughout a trial and will wield a great deal of power in deciding objections and motions as they are raised by the lawyers, the only proactive role a judge has in a trail is to keep an orderly courtroom environment and to give the instruction to the jury before it retires to deliberate. During the instruction, the judge will clarify matters of law for the jurors, such as which party has the burden of proving a particular point or what specific charges they will be deciding. Even the jury instruction, however, is not the sole purview of the judge, as it will be heavily influenced by the attorneys as they object to particular pieces before it is ever read to a jury. Thus, in American jurisprudence, unless the judge is not only the trier of law but also the trier of fact (the final decision maker in a nonjury trial), he or she has three main duties: to maintain a level playing field, to arbitrate disagreements between the combatants as they arise, and to give guidance to the jury so that it can reach its ultimate decision as to who will emerge victorious.

In legal cinema, although we see judges perform all three of these duties, we see them working to keep courtroom order and ruling on objections and motions far more than we ever see them instruct the jury. Sometimes judges assert their authority to keep order even before any distraction takes place, as in *Ghosts of Mississippi*, where the judge warns, "When the verdict is read, there will be no demonstrations or emotional outbursts of any type." Similarly, Judge Weaver in *Anatomy of a Murder* says, "I warn all those present not to interrupt the taking of the verdict. I will stop the proceedings and clear the courtroom if there is any demonstration." Earlier in the proceedings he stops the trial to tell the courtroom about a pair of panties that will be discussed, warning the spectators directly, "I wanted you to get your snickering over and done with. This pair of panties will be mentioned again in the course of this trial. And when it happens, there will be not one laugh, one snicker, one giggle or even one smirk in my courtroom." The first shot of Judge

Clark Carrigan, played by John Dehner, in *Jagged Edge* is a zoom to the judge behind his desk in chambers, saying to the lawyers, "I'm telling you now, I see this trial degenerating and I'll hit you like a freight train roaring down the High Sierra. We have a man's life at stake here, not headlines, not careers." In almost the exact same type of shot, Judge Irwin Silver, played by J. S. Block, in *Music Box* first appears in a zoom into a close-up of his opening the trial by saying calmly but sternly, "I will tolerate no outbursts, disturbances or interruptions." Judge Silver keeps both the gallery and the lawyers in line, as when he tells the zealous prosecutor, "Mr. Burke, in this courtroom, address your questions to me, not to opposing counsel."

Most of the time, judges are shown keeping order as the trial is in progress. In *Chicago*, as the film cuts back and forth between the "Razzle Dazzle" musical number taking place under the big top and the merely metaphorical circus taking place in the courtroom during the trial of Roxie Hart for the murder of her lover, the judge is shown trying to keep order and being mostly unsuccessful. Judge Sylvia Waxman in *Wild Things* is not beyond scolding lawyers or even the district attorney (played with appropriate pomposity by Robert Wagner), who objects from the gallery in a case that is being handled by his office but not specifically by him. Judge Waxman glares at him and says, "Mr. Baxter, you are not trying this case. Sit down!"

Often in legal cinema, the prop used to show a judge attempting to assert courtroom decorum is the gavel. During the courtroom finale of the original *Miracle on 34th Street*, the judge manages to keep hitting his gavel even as thousands of letters to Santa are poured onto his desk to prove that the Kris Kringle on trial for his sanity is indeed "the one and only Santa Claus." Judge Atkins in *Kramer vs. Kramer* bangs his gavel and warns Dustin Hoffman's client character, who is yelling and evading difficult questions on the witness stand, "Mr. Kramer, I must urge you to stop or else I'll have to hold you in contempt!" In *The Devil's Advocate*, the judge stands and furiously pounds his gavel as the father of a molestation victim leaps to attack the lawyer defending the abuser. The judge here even threatens the entire gallery audience with contempt. Judge Bean in the legal western *The Life and Times of Judge Roy Bean* increases his effectiveness by using a gun as a gavel.

The inability of the judge to keep order is sometimes used for comic effect. A montage of three judges, for example, is used in the legal comedy *Laws of Attraction* to show the increasingly bitter competition between the two bickering lawyers played by Julianne Moore and Pierce Brosnan. In *Trial and Error*, when the ever-amusing Austin Pendleton (who also plays a lawyer in *My Cousin Vinny*) as Judge Paul Graff yells, "I will have order in my court!" it is followed by a lawyer played by Jeff Daniels crashing through the ceiling onto the floor of the courtroom in a cloud of dust and debris. A similar comic moment of courtroom chaos occurs in *Intolerable Cruelty*, when the defendant lunges at a witness and the opposing lawyer stands up and says, "Objection, your honor! Strangling the witness!" The judge, obviously sharing the audience's opinion of the annoying, prissy witness Heinz, the Baron Krauss von Espy, says, as she has for most of the objections raised during the trial, "I'm going to allow it."

Judges are shown ruling on objections or motions in just about every film in which they appear. Before we even see an image in *Guilty as Sin*, we hear a gavel and a judge saying, "sustained" to some unheard and unseen objection. The only courtroom action at all in *Erin Brockovich* is that of Judge LeRoy A. Simmons playing himself as he matter-of-factly dismisses all 84 motions to strike down and demur the charges brought against the corporate giant PG&E, saying to their lawyers, "Tell your clients they are going to trial." Michael Douglas in *The Star Chamber* is shown twice ruling on motions about the propriety of searches and the evidence they uncover. His decisions on those motions amount to a verdict on the cases themselves: If the evidence is admitted, the accused will be found guilty, and if excluded they will go free. Judge Weaver in *Anatomy of a Murder* takes a long, deliberate pause in the middle of a trial to rule on a motion of whether to allow a particular line of questioning that everyone in the court knows will probably determine the outcome of the case. In *A Time to Kill*, Judge Omar Noose lives up to his hanging judge moniker when he denies the motion for a change of venue without even giving the defense a chance to submit a brief to support the motion. The judge is eventually forced to reconsider and allow for briefs to be proffered but still denies the motion to move the trial to a locale where a fair trial will be possible. Incredibly, the trial proceeds even with the Ku Klux Klan rioting outside the courthouse within earshot of the jury and a sniper taking out a National Guardsman who was supposed to protect both the protesting crowds and the defendant.

Perhaps because the movie is based on an actual case, *A Civil Action* uncharacteristically pays a great deal of attention to the instruction that will be given to the jury by John Lithgow as the somewhat erratic Judge Walter J. Skinner. The judge devises an unusual way for the jury to render its verdict: Rather than having the jury find for the plaintiffs or defendants in the traditional up-or-down manner, Judge Skinner creates factual questions for the jury to answer that will decide the outcome of the case. When John Travolta as the plaintiff's lawyer Jan Schlichtmann complains in chambers of the confusing and overly technical wording of the questions, the judge yells, "Enough!" Although *Twelve Angry Men* also begins with a judge giving his instruction to the jury before it retires to deliberate, *A Civil Action* is not only one of the few films to show in any detail how a judge's jury instruction evolves but also appears to be the only film in the history of legal cinema to make the delivery of a jury instruction a major plot point in the movie.

In general, movies seem to portray judges as standing for justice itself. For example, the judge in *JFK* is often represented not so much as a real person but as an unseen booming voice with a hammering gavel. Paul Newman as the title character in *The Life and Times of Judge Roy Bean* makes no distinction between himself as the judge and the law itself. "I am the new law in this area," he says. "The law west of the Pecos." In referring to how he will protect the Mexican town folk in his area, he says, "The law is going to protect them." Later, draped in the flag of Texas as his judicial robe, he says to an outlaw attempting to cite *The Laws and Statutes of the State of Texas*, "You're gonna hang no matter what it says in there because I am the law."

Most often, the judge is cinematically portrayed as the ideal of powerful justice, where the neutral but powerful judge will assure at least a level playing field, if not always a fair outcome. In *Guilty as Sin*, we see "In God We Trust" in the background behind and over Judge Tompkins, played by Dana Ivey, as if to remind the audience that God, justice, and the judge are to be trusted implicitly. Interestingly, the first judge to hear Claudia's sanity case in *Nuts* also sits below a very visible "In God We Trust" as does Judge Abromovitz played by Nora Dunn in *Laws of Attraction.* In *The Hurricane,* the judge who first sentences Rubin Carter to three life sentences for murders Rubin did not commit sits below the seal of the United States, as does the federal Judge Sarokin, played memorably by Rod Steiger, who will eventually set Rubin free decades later.

Steiger's Judge Sarokin is also shot exclusively from a lower angle, using the composition of the shot to put the law quite literally on a pedestal and thus elevating the judge to a position of extra importance. Likewise, in the trial near the conclusion of *Mrs. Doubtfire,* in which Daniel Hillard, played by Robin Williams, pleads for custody of his children, the judge is shot exclusively from below, looking quite serious, when he allows for only court-supervised weekly child visitation for the devoted, sympathetic father. The stern judge at the beginning of *Carlito's Way* is also shot from below. Interestingly, the judge in *The Untouchables,* played by Tony Mockus, Sr., and listed in the credits only as "Judge," is shown from below until the audience discovers that he has received bribes. As our hero Eliot Ness is about the confront him with that fact in chambers, the judge is shown for the first time from above, looking far less powerful than he did in court when shown from a low camera angle. He is again shot meekly from above when the film cuts back to him on the bench, disgraced and head in hands. He only reclaims his rightful place on the pedestal of respectability and is shot again from below when he does the right thing and orders the bailiff to replace the jury that has been bribed with the untainted jury from another trial.

Even when judges are portrayed in a fictional future, they are shown as the protective firewall standing between citizens and either anarchy or corruption. In the third-millennium world of *Judge Dredd,* for example, where a parched planet has led to severely overcrowded cities and gangs of street savages wreaking havoc, it is "The Judges" who are the only hope for order. So what if these judges, a combination of police, jury, and executioner, are only a step above the violence they seek to quell? They equate killing with judging, performing "summary executions" rather than just summary judgments. When the title character, played by Sylvester Stallone, arrives at a "block war" and tells the marauding crowd, "Here I am: The Law! Throw down your weapons and prepare to be judged," he means surrender or get shot and killed. After shooting the last rioter, Dredd deadpans, "Court dismissed." Still, these judges want to stand for "freedom not oppression," as articulated by Chief Justice Fargo, played by the always imposing Max von Sydow. Even the cold and brutal Dredd is described by another character as worshipping the law and is shown this way cinematically when he stands before an ancient statute of justice, music swelling, like a gladiator standing to salute a Roman god. Similarly, when the police detective in *Minority Report,* played by Tom Cruise, is about to make an arrest in the future world of "precrime," where perpetrators are arrested before they commit their murders, he must first get the approval of the chief judge, who is waiting via video conference call to authorize the arrest. "Affirmative, I will validate," is the command the judge gives before the police spring into action. Even in this supposedly perfect system, where crime is prevented before it even happens on the basis of the psychic visions of "precogs" who can see murders before they occur, the judge is shown as the true protector of justice—the necessary safety measure to keep the law fair.

However, legal cinema is not kind to those judges who make the mistake of confusing themselves with being the law rather than simply the guarantor of a fair forum in which the law can be argued. For example, in *Judge Dredd,* the opening narration, punctuated by the ponderous voice of James Earl Jones, tells us that these judges of the future are, "a force with the power to dispense both justice and punishment." Judge Dredd is not far off then when he exclaims to a tribunal of judges, "I am the law!" For his audacity, the film immediately sends Dredd to the Denver Penal Colony. Even Chief Justice Fargo knows this arrangement is dangerous, as when he confesses to Dredd on his deathbed, looking at a statute of justice, "Justice. Before your time. We should never have taken justice out of her hands.... Too much power in one person's hands."

Characters in *The Life and Times of Judge Roy Bean* accurately refer to the hanging judge who never has a jury and basically makes the law up as he goes along as an "egomaniac" and a "two-bit, vigilante judge." He gets to the point where he rips a page out of a statute book because he does not like a law that would give his town away in a land grab, saying, "I just repealed it." Later, he is voted out of his position for not being responsive to the people he was supposed to protect.

Likewise, in *The Star Chamber*, Hal Holbrook as Judge Caulfield tells the newly appointed Judge Hardin that, "We're the goddamned law! . . . We're the judges, for Christ's sake. We're the law!" The audience is shown the unsavory extension of that philosophy when it learns of the clandestine tribunal of judges that, after real trials are concluded, dispenses its own vigilante justice on the cases that its members view as perversions of the law. "Our own court of last resort," Judge Caulfield explains. This scheme, which is at first presented as an appealing prospect in a system that customary lets heinous criminals go free, is ultimately exposed as dangerous. A plot twist reveals that the judges have mistakenly come to a guilty verdict that will result in the accused being killed for crimes they did not commit. "I can't help feeling we've become them," Judge Hardin says to his Star Chamber colleagues. Here another legal film shows its suspicion of having the power of judge, jury, and executioner residing in only one person or group of people.

Most often when they are shown in movies, judges are portrayed as the audience would probably like to think of them: strict, perhaps even hard applicators of the law, the voice of stern yet fair justice. The judge in *Runaway Jury*, for example, played by Bruce McGill (the same actor who played Sheriff Farley in *My Cousin Vinny*) runs a tight ship and is also civic minded. He loses patience with potential juror Nick Easter, played by John Cusack, when Easter tries to get out of jury duty. The judge in *Inherit the Wind*, played by Harry Morgan, is kind enough to comfort an upset witness and tough enough to put the defendant's lawyer in jail for contempt. In the end, he is forgiving and merciful in sentencing the high school teacher found guilty of teaching evolution to only a fine of $100. Alfre Woodard is the tough, matter-of-fact judge in *Primal Fear* who quiets the gallery when audience members so much as gasp and later fines one of the lawyers $10,000 for contempt and even threatens to have him disbarred. She runs an efficient trial despite (or thanks to?) drinking large quantities of straight whisky in her chambers. Judge Stanley Murdoch, played by James Whitmore, in *Nuts* is understanding, compassionate, patient, and accommodating, but he also runs the courtroom by the book and is always conscious of the need to move things along. Similarly, the female judge at Sam's first hearing in *I Am Sam* tries to be very understanding to the mentally disabled man appearing before her, but she is also tough as she tries to move along a busy court docket of cases.

The aforementioned Judge Irwin Silver from *Music Box*, played by J. S. Block, is suspected of being affected by his Jewish heritage in a trail involving Nazi war crimes. The lawyers speculate whether he will bend over backward to be fair. One lawyer points out the influence that public opinion can have on the judge, telling defense attorney Ann Talbot, played by Jessica Lange, that, "The world will be your jury. Even paragons of virtue like Judge Silver are human beings." But the judge is both even-keeled and even in his distribution of justice. He remains calm, even when lawyers are yelling at each other, simply calling them to the bench. When a piece of new evidence arrives from the Hungarian government, he lets defense counsel's forensic examiners scrutinize the document before the Justice Department does. By giving the judge a substantial amount of screen time and always showing him to be fair, tough, neutral, and calm, the filmmakers provide the audience with a very satisfying picture of balanced justice.

Sometimes the audience is tricked into thinking the judge will be so strict as to be unfair to the client or his or her lawyer, only to find out that the judge is both stern and fair. In his last film role in the vastly underrated courtroom comedy *My Cousin Vinny*, Fred Gwynne impeccably plays Judge Chamberlain Haller. For much of the film, he is Vinny's nemesis. A serious Yale graduate and a formal, self-confessed stickler for procedure, the judge is so intelligent, he plays himself in chess. Before trial, he gives Vinny a copy of the huge *Alabama Rules of Criminal Procedure* and warns the out-of-state lawyer that he will be given no leeway. The judge holds Vinny in contempt during his first appearance for not giving a simple "guilty" or "not guilty" plea. He appears to have almost a vendetta against Vinny, holding him in contempt and imprisoning him a total of three times, investigating the prior trial work Vinny claims to have done in New York, and denying Vinny's request for a one-day continuance to prepare for the examination of a surprise witness introduced by the prosecution. Throughout the trial, however, the judge is still fair to the defendants, and in the end he comes to like and respect Vinny, telling him, "I am honored to shake your hand. . . . You're one hell of a trial lawyer."

Similarly, ex-Marine drill sergeant R. Lee Ermey, introduced to audiences in Stanley Kubrick's *Full Metal Jacket*, plays Judge Clawson in *Murder in the First*. He is very tough—even mean—giving the newly appointed public defender, played by Christian Slater, only a one-week continuance to prepare for the case. He later yells at the young lawyer, accusing him of trying the case in the media instead of in court. Judge Clawson twice threatens the public defender with contempt, once yelling at the top of his lungs (which, as those familiar with Ermey know, is saying something). Still, the judge also yells at the prosecution and tells the district attorney to "Shut up!" In the ultimate act of fairness, and perhaps even deference to the defense, the judge overrules the prosecution's objection and lets the defense put Alcatraz and its cruel conditions on trial. Instead of ending the trial (and the movie) by sustaining the prosecution's motion, the judge is shown as a boisterous, stern, but ultimately fair arbitrator.

Sometimes judges in films are strict but conduct themselves in the court with a sort of folksy charm. For some reason, the majority of the time these folksy but stern judges are portrayed by African American actors. The archetype is probably Ossie Davis's amusing portrayal of Judge Harry Roosevelt in *The Client*. Judge Roosevelt is not hampered by formality or by the expectations of how a judge is supposed to act. He makes his own fishing lures in his chambers (perhaps in an homage to the small town, folksy, lure-making lawyer played by James Stewart in *Anatomy of a Murder*). He knows scripture even better than the U.S. attorney appearing before him (played by Tommy Lee Jones), who has been given the nickname "Reverend Roy" because of his penchant for, and expertise in, quoting the Bible. The judge corrects Roy when he misquotes Psalms, telling him that the passage he has recited is from Proverbs, and gives it to him literally chapter and verse. But one would be foolish to mistake Judge Roosevelt's folksiness as softness. He has no compunction about dismissing from his court before the hearing begins both a police officer wearing a sidearm and a reporter. He scolds a U.S. attorney (played by Bradley Whitford) for standing and speaking before he is addressed and then scolds Whitford's boss as well. However, even in his scolding, the judge has a irreverent humor and a down-to-earth demeanor: "Rule Number One: You will speak only when spoken to. Rule Number Two: Do not grace his honor with unsolicited commentary. Rule Number Three: His honor does not like to listen to the voices of U.S. attorneys who love to hear themselves speak." The normally imposing Reverend Roy can only respond like a soldier before a superior in the military: "Sir, yes sir." The sequence is supremely satisfying to the audience, seeing the ambitious, ruthless, and normally self-assured Reverend Roy, who has been in total control of the case—even to the point of bullying the 11-year-old child client—humbled by the power of the law as personified in this stern, confident judge who can be tough and yet completely without arrogance.

Similar to the Ossie Davis folksy-but-stern model of the cinematic judge is Paul Winfield as Judge Larren Lyttle in *Presumed Innocent*. He too is African American, humorous, and tough and no-nonsense. At one point, he warns a lawyer, "Mr. Stern, you are playing with fire." Like many judges, he is always shot from below, with the camera looking up at this personification of the rule of law. We also come to learn that he has an interesting back story—a history of having taken bribes as a prosecutor during a period of depression, provoked by the death of his wife, when he was drinking heavily. Still, he is referred to by the character who discusses these past transgressions as "a distinguished mind and a career that does honor to the bench." Danny Glover, another African American actor, in an uncredited part in *The Rainmaker* plays newly appointed Judge Tyrone Kipler. He is down-to-earth enough to go to the home of a poor, ailing witness to get his testimony before the young man dies, and suggests holding the deposition outside in the yard, where it will be less cramped. Earlier, in chambers, he asks the brand-new plaintiff counsel, Rudy Baylor, played by Matt Damon, "You in over your head, son?" The green lawyer confidently replies, "Absolutely," making the judge smile in a folksy—even fatherly—kind of way. Still, Judge Kipler is tough and fair, scolding Rudy for not asking permission before approaching a witness, tapping his watch reproachfully when Rudy shows up late for court, and responding to Rudy's excuse for not alerting opposing counsel to a surprise witness ("It's my first trial.") by saying sharply, "Not good enough." The judge in *Liar Liar* is Marshall Stevens, another African American judge, this time played by Jason Bernard. Similar to the others, he is stern but tempers his strict manner with wit. When lawyer Fletcher Reede, played by Jim Carrey, is forced by his son's birthday wish to tell the truth for twenty-four hours, Carrey responds to the judge's inquiry at the beginning of the trial as to how he is doing by answering truthfully but embarrassingly, "I'm a little upset about a bad sexual episode I had last night." Without batting an eye, Judge Stevens says, "Well, you're still young. It will happen more and more. In the meantime, what do you say we get down to business?" *Legal Eagles* also features a stern African American judge with a keen comic timing, played by veteran character actor Roscoe Lee Browne.

Although there is a strange predominance of African American actors playing tough, folksy judges, there are some Caucasian folksy types as well. Judge Taylor in *To Kill a Mockingbird* is presumably no relation to TV's Andy Taylor, but he is just as neighborly, as would be expected in the story's small-town, long-ago setting. Paul Fix, who plays the judge, even visits Atticus personally on his porch one warm evening to assign him the difficult case of defending an innocent Black man accused of raping a White girl. Unlike the other folksy judges, however, he is not humorous, only fair and neutral. The only sign of his humanity comes after the unfair guilty verdict is read and the trial concluded, when he exits the courtroom and slams the door to his chambers in apparent disgust. Judge Weaver in *Anatomy of a Murder* is a more traditional folksy judge, going back and forth from stern to lighthearted. He begins his trial by informing the courtroom, "While I may appear to doze [on the bench] occasionally, you'll find that I'm easily awakened, particularly if shaken gently by a good lawyer with a nice point of law." He later gently scolds a witness who has elicited laughter in the courtroom, saying, "Just answer the questions, Mr. Paquette. The attorneys will provide the wisecracks." In allowing one of the lawyers to present a dog as evidence in the trial, the judge says, "A creature who cannot talk will be a welcome relief." Still, the judge is portrayed as tough, threatening one of the lawyers

(Jimmy Stewart, no less) with contempt for an outburst in court. Another time he warns the lawyers, "The next one to speak out of turn will have me to deal with." Joseph N. Welch, the actor playing Judge Weaver, has a slow, deliberate style of acting that borders on the awkward. This is explained by a fascinating piece of casting by the film's director, Otto Preminger. Welch was a real-life lawyer—the same Mr. Welch who, when defending the army against Senator McCarthy in the infamous communist hearings, uttered what playwright Tony Kushner dubbed in *Angels in America* "the greatest punchline in American history,"[5] the famous line that began the end of the committee's reign of terror: "Have you no decency, sir? At long last, have you no sense of decency?"[6]

Sometimes judges are shown in legal cinema as downtrodden and world weary, appearing to have had contact with too many courtroom antics, loathsome clients, and misapplications of justice in their careers in the law. The judge seen briefly at the start of *Twelve Angry Men*, for example, plays absentmindedly with a pencil as he mumbles his instruction to the jury, concluding by leaning his cheek against his hand and saying unconvincingly in one breath, "You are faced with a grave responsibility, thank you, gentlemen." It could be the severe heat that the jurors complain about later on, but it appears equally as likely that this is the hundredth time this judge has delivered this instruction to yet another jury in what has become just another case. The judge in *JFK* appears similarly nonchalant and exhausted. He enters court smoking a cigarette and is shown smoking later during the government's closing argument. He seems exasperated with the crusading district attorney Jim Garrison (Kevin Costner), sustaining just about all of the defense's objections, and at one point literally holding his head in his hands as if at the end of his rope. Judge Harvey Hale in *The Rainmaker*, played by Dean Stockwell, freely admits to the lawyer played by Matt Damon, who is suing an insurance company on behalf of a young man dying of leukemia, "I'm really tired of these types of lawsuits. I'm inclined to grant the motion to dismiss.... I don't want it clogging up my docket." Even this rookie lawyer, however, recognizes the judge for what he is when he tells another character, "He's just an old, angry man who's been sitting on that bench too long."

The federal judge portrayed by Rod Steiger in *The Hurricane* appears fully present and involved in the trial, until immediately after setting Rubin Carter free we see him nonchalantly look at his watch à la George H. W. Bush. Are the filmmakers implying that this defining moment in Carter's life, which has been decades in the making, is just another day at work for the judge or, worse, that he has better things he would rather be doing? (Or is it the trademark eccentricity of Rod Steiger as an actor that the filmmakers leave in for fun?) Similarly, is the frequent drinking on the job of Alfre Woodard's judge in *Primal Fear* a salve for too many years on the bench, seeing too many grandstanding lawyers, scumbag clients and other twistings of justice? Jack Warden's Judge Rayford in ... *And Justice for All* appears to have gone a step beyond uncaring to the point of insanity because of all the strangeness that has come before him as a judge. He lunches on the ledge outside his chamber window on an upper floor of the courthouse. In the middle of court, he attempts to calm the lawyers by shooting a pistol into the air and then calmly saying, "Gentlemen, need I remind you, you are in a court of law?" Later he explains, "There's law and there's order. This," he says pointing to his gun, "is order." He flies helicopters and goes past the halfway point of his fuel reserves to see whether he can make it back on the fumes. And at one point, while on recess from a trial, he unsuccessfully tries to swallow the muzzle of a rifle in an apparent suicide. All in all, Judge Rayford appears beyond sanity—and certainly beyond the point of having faith in the law or in his ability to do justice.

Occasionally, the judge in legal cinema is portrayed as at least biased and at worst corrupt, overseeing a fixed game from the start. Sometimes the judges' transgressions are huge—even criminal. More often, they are simply suspect but nonetheless leave the audience with the distinct impression that the case being tried before the judge is not playing out in a perfectly equal forum or being adjudicated by a truly impartial referee.

On the less egregious end of the spectrum of judges with compromised neutrality are those who are cozier with one side than the other. John Lithgow's Judge Skinner in *A Civil Action* is chummy with the defendant's corporate lawyers before the trial even begins. After Robert Duvall, as one of the defendant lawyers, tells plaintiff's counsel that the lawyer will never get his victimized clients onto the witness stand, the judge adopts the very plan hatched by Duvall's Jerry Facher to keep the families from testifying. When the plantiff's attorney confronts the judge on giving in to the plan, the judge screams defensively, "It's my plan!" Likewise, the judge in *A Time to Kill*, played by Patrick McGoohan, can be seen walking and laughing outside of court with the district attorney even as the trial is in recess, which probably constitutes a technically illegal *ex parte* communication. *The Rainmaker* has at least slightly biased judges on either side of a case. Judge Hale, played by Dean Stockwell, is cozy enough with the insurance company's lawyer, Leo Drummond, played by Jon Voight, that the judge orchestrates a tag team in chambers during which Drummond can pitch a settlement to the plaintiff's lawyer and the judge can push it, saying, "You'd be crazy not the take that [settlement]." After Judge Hale dies, the case is assigned to Judge Tyrone Kipler, played by Danny Glover, who is described by "paralawyer" Deck Shifflet, played by Danny DeVito, as hating Drummond and his law firm and as "tough on insurance companies, sues them all the time. Great luck for us, kid!" Later on, when the judge is happily forced by precedent to reverse a prior ruling and rule against the defendant's motion, he smiles (barely containing a chuckle) and says to Drummond, "Sorry Leo." Drummond replies sarcastically, "Oh, I'm sure you are, your honor!"

Milo O'Shea as Judge Hoyle in *The Verdict* is not only biased against Paul Newman's Frank Galvin as a plaintiff's lawyer in a medical malpractice suit, he is also lazy and resents it when the lawyer forces him to do any work, including spending extra time in court. Newman, in one of the movie's climatic scenes finally confronts the judge in chambers, saying, "They said you're a hard ass, you're a defendant's judge.... You couldn't hack it as a lawyer. You were a bagman for the boys downtown, and you're still one!" From the very beginning, the judge seems to be against Newman's character. In chambers, when Newman arrives as the judge and defendant's lawyer are already chatting and laughing, the judge pushes a settlement apparently to avoid the work and inconvenience of a trial, saying, "This case should never have come to trial." He shows displeasure when Newman declines the invitation to break off questioning so they can go to lunch. He will not grant an extension when the plaintiff's witness disappears, saying coldly, "I have no sympathy for you," before literally closing a door in the lawyer's face. Most startling, at one point in the trial the judge actually rises and asks the witness a question, quite improperly doing the job of the defendant's lawyer and indicating to the jury just whose side he is on. Even when Newman receives the verdict in his client's favor, the judge seems to be in pain when he must tell the jury in response to their question that they are not limited to the award amount requested by the plaintiff.

The judge in *Chicago* is shown not so much as exhibiting favoritism to the defendants as being seduced along with the jury and the rest of the judicial system by the razzle-dazzle of attorney Billy Flynn and the sensation surrounding his murdering female clients. During the musical number that sandwiches scenes from the actual trial of Roxie Hart, blind justice is on a trapeze, and the judge and jury have circus showgirls teasing them into distraction as Billy sings, "How can they see with sequins in their eyes? . . . How can they hear the truth above the roar?" The judge may not be crooked, but he is portrayed as at the least being easily bamboozled.

Two films in legal cinema (well, one film and its remake) point out that political considerations can have an effect on the impartiality of a judge. Judge Henry Harper, in both the original 1947 *Miracle on 34th Street* and the 1994 remake, is up for reelection—a fact that enters into the trial of Kris Kringle. In the 1994 version, Robert Prosky as Judge Harper makes a hint about a campaign contribution from the district attorney before signing Kris's commitment papers, saying, "Money makes the world go round." He does not appear to be soliciting a bribe, but he does not appear to be above being influenced by a gesture in support of his reelection, either. In the original version of the film, the political difficulties are more clearly spelled out. Gene Lockhart's Judge Harper has a hired political consultant (William Frawley in a crusty role straight out of Tammany Hall), who tells him that if he rules that there is no Santa Claus, "You can count on getting just two votes: your own and that district attorney's out there." The judge, however, is principled and honest and will not dodge the case despite his campaign manager's recommendation. Still, he is not above being overly deferential to Kris and being cleverly diplomatic in ruling that on the question of whether there is a Santa Claus, "The court therefore intends to keep an open mind. We shall hear evidence from both sides." In this case, politics have not led to an unfair judge, but they have created one who is particularly careful.

Farther down the spectrum of unfair judges are those who are prejudiced and who appear to be more willing to play to racial biases than do their duty to provide a fair trial. For example, in *Ghosts of Mississippi*, we find out that the judge in the original trial of the man accused of assassinating civil rights leader Medgar Evers, which resulted in a hung jury, kept the murder weapon as a souvenir after the trial was over. If he was not proud to obtain the rifle that supposedly killed the crusading Black man, he at the very least was guilty of stealing evidence that might be needed in a later trial or appeal, particularly given the hung jury in the original trial. That same judge allowed for a former governor to enter the courtroom and shake the hand of the defendant while the trial is going on and the victim's widow is testifying on the stand. A reporter observes, "There's not a court in America that would stand for that." A colleague responds, "What does America got to do with anything? This is Mississippi."

We more starkly see the racial bias of a judge in the brief trial sequence in the middle of *Mississippi Burning*. Here, when a group of men plead guilty to bombing the home of a Black family to discourage them and their neighbors from registering to vote, the judge gives them only a suspended sentence of five years, saying, "The court understands . . . without condoning, mind you, how your actions were provoked" by "outside agitators . . . of low morality"; namely, the FBI. As is often the case in legal cinema, the film attempts to show that when the judge is compromised or tainted, all hope of justice is lost. It is his verdict that spurs the FBI, out of frustration, into more unconventional and hard-hitting tactics.

One of the worst types of judge in legal cinema appears to be the bribed or otherwise crooked judge. In *The Untouchables*, in addition to the aforementioned judge who comes around only after Eliot Ness threatens to expose him as being on the take, there appears to be a whole category of "Federal Circuit Judges" in Capone's ledger book who have been corrupted by payoffs. When Demi Moore, as the title character in *The Juror*, goes to the judge during the case of a mob boss accused of murder to tell the judge that she and her son are being threatened, he telegraphs to her that it is too late for him to help. "Are you telling me I'm making a mistake?" she asks after going to him for help but then realizing that he has been "gotten to," either by a bribe or by mob threats. He is almost angry with her for putting him in an awkward and presumably dangerous position. "I gave you every opportunity to get out of serving on this jury," he says. "But you insisted! You wanted jury duty! Do you recall?" In *Angels with Dirty Faces*, all the court action is played off screen and relayed to the viewer through newspaper headlines that scream the developments in the case against William "Rocky" Sullivan, played to perfection by James Cagney. Still, the audience is told that judges are on the take, being blackmailed, or having their careers or lives threatened. In his radio address confronting the city corruption being perpetrated by his childhood friend Rocky and his gangland colleagues, the crusading Father Connolly, played with saintly charm by Pat O'Brien, asks, "What political sword does he hold over the trembling hands of DAs and judges?" Father Connolly understands that when you are dealing with crooked or hamstrung judges, desperate measures are called for.

Finally, there are the lowest of low judges in legal cinema—the criminal judges, judges who have perpetrated some crime and who are attempting to get away with it. In these films, similar to how the presumption of the innocent client is used to surprise and trick the audience, the presumption of the judge as a fair keeper of the law is used to provide a surprise plot twist for the audience.

In . . . *And Justice for All*, for example, John Forsythe's hard-assed Judge Fleming is guilty of brutally beating and raping a woman but basically forces attorney Arthur Kirkland to defend him and get him cleared of the crime. The audience is dubious about Fleming's guilt after having been told by some cops early in the film that Fleming "hates scum almost as much as we do," and after having been treated to seeing the judge tell an accused defendant before him in court, "You are also a revolting, despicable scum of the earth who should be taken out and squashed like a cockroach." Yet his guilt is established when Kirkland is presented with kinky photos of the judge—photos that he cannot reveal because of attorney/ client privilege. Judge Fleming even manages to get a polygraph test falsified for his lawyer. His brutality and hypocrisy are added to with revulsion, as when he whispers to Arthur about his rape victim, "I wouldn't mind seeing her again sometime." The crisis of conscience for Arthur of having to defend a loathsome, guilty judge finally leads to his famous "You're out of order" courtroom breakdown, which ends with him tearfully scolding Judge Fleming, "You're supposed to stand for something! You're supposed to protect people!"

The entire success of *Suspect* depends on the surprise twist of the judge turning out to be a ruthless murderer. John Mahoney plays Judge Matthew Helms opposite Cher's attorney Kathleen Riley. Like Fleming in... *And Justice for All,* Helms is an inflexible, unreasonable judge who constantly overrules Kathleen's objections and motions. At one point he hisses at her in open court, "One more stunt like that, counselor, and I'll slap you with a contempt citation so fast you won't know what hit you!" Later on, we find out why: Kathleen's client has been framed by Judge Helms for a murder the judge committed to silence a woman who, just as he was up for appointment to a U.S. circuit court, discovered that he once conspired to fix a case. The surprise revelation of the murdering judge sets up the film's finale thriller chase, with Helms now seeking to murder Kathleen before juror Dennis Quaid can come to her rescue. Even considering the strained plausibility of the plot, the movie stands for the premise that a blatantly unfair judge, never mind a criminal one, is indeed a rare thing in legal cinema. Thus, the filmmakers have the makings of what is intended to be a neat surprise ending.

Once in a great while, judges are shown as meek and almost invisible, perhaps to indicate a true neutrality. In *Nell,* for example, the judge is unseen for most of the first hearing, when the two doctors are arguing about what the best course of action is for the "wild child" recently found secluded in a woodland cabin. When the judge is seen, it is to give his Solomon-like ruling that the two doctors should observe Nell together for three months to better inform the court as to a course of action. Later on, the judge further fleshes out his fairness when he is shown as kind and gentle with Nell and even allows her to address the court directly, albeit with her doctor acting as an interpreter of the unique language shared only by Nell, her dead sister, her mother, and now her two doctors. Similarly, the female Judge Tate in *Philadelphia* is seen only infrequently and often silently. She is calm and matter-of-fact even when things get testy and is soft-spoken but stern in responding to objections. The only show of emotion or bias she displays is in the subtle raising of an eyebrow (literally) when she sees the lesions on the body of plaintiff Andrew Beckett after he removes his shirt on the witness stand in court. Because of the almost invisibility of the judge, the audience can never suspect that Andrew is getting anything less than a fair trial.

Other times, the diminished presence of the judge might indicate a failing of the legal system, one in which the rule of law has failed to fully protect the innocent or in which the judge has failed to be a zealous protector of the law. In *The Accused*, for example, the judge is shown only matter-of-factly, even quietly uttering common courtroom phrases like, "state your name" and, "please be seated." He is often shown in long shot, looking meek and small behind the bench. This adds to the feeling of revictimization for gang-rape survivor Sarah Tobias, played by Jodie Foster. The judge is not so much there to provide justice to the woman who has been wronged but to allow society to continue with its practice (then) of minimizing rape and putting the victim on trial, even indirectly. Similarly, Henry Fonda as *The Wrong Man* cannot depend on the judge to save him from the injustice to which he is being subjected as the victim of a mistaken identity. The judge at arraignment is practically unseen, with Hitchcock's camera shooting from over the judge's left shoulder. At trial, the judge does not get much better exposure: He is first seen in long shot from the back of the courtroom, and throughout the trial, he is shown exclusively either in the distance or in the background.

In *New Jack City*, in which the vicious gang lord Nino Brown, played by Wesley Snipes, is about to cop a plea and receive only one year in jail in exchange for giving up his contacts, the judge is seen and heard from only twice: when banging the gavel and saying, "Order in the court," and then when accepting the plea and delivering the sentence, saying, "The court is unhappy with this application." The absent judge symbolizes the absence of justice for Nino's murdered victims and the lives ruined by his drug trade.

In summation, then, the judge in legal cinema, whether ruling on motions or objections or working to keep order in the court, generally goes about his or her duties in one of four distinct ways: strictly and sternly, with a folksy charm, wearily and cynically, or sometimes corrupted by greed or another nefarious motivation. This last category is the exception rather than the rule. In those few instances in which the judge is shown as corrupt, bigoted, or otherwise immoral, it is done to indicate to the audience that the legal system—and often society itself—is quite broken and that something drastic needs to change. A crooked judge, even more than an unfair jury verdict, seems to indicate that all hope of justice is gone and that the rule of law itself has been perverted. The neutral referee role of the judge necessary for the even application of justice is apparently understood and valued by the audience and is thus reflected by filmmakers throughout the breadth of legal cinema.

3

Trial of One's Peers: The Jury

"This I have always thought is a remarkable thing about democracy. We are . . . notified by mail to come down to this place to decide on the guilt or innocence of a man we have never heard of before. We have nothing to gain or lose by our verdict. This is one of the reasons why we are strong."
—George Voskovec as Juror #11 in *Twelve Angry Men*

"Twelve people go off into a room. Twelve different minds, twelve different hearts, twelve different walks of life. Twelve sets of eyes, ears, shapes and sizes. And these twelve people are asked to judge another human being as different from them as they are from each other. And in their judgment they must become of one mind . . . unanimous. That's one of the miracles of man's disorganized soul that they can do it, and in most instances do it right well. God bless juries!"
—Arthur O'Connell as Parnell Emmett McCarthy in *Anatomy of a Murder*

Although it may sound oxymoronic, in the drama of the legal cinema, the jury is the silent Greek chorus. Nowhere is the conscience of the audience, and thus society as a whole, more represented in film than in the jury, even if it is done so for the most part in a very subtle way. The lawyer may represent our ideal crusader, the victim may stand for the downtrodden in society, and the judge may symbolize the cold but firm power of the law, but the people and their societal sense of right and wrong are given voice in the cinematic trial through the jury.

In *Murder in the First*, for example, the public defender, played by Christian Slater, has been claiming throughout the trial that the staff at Alcatraz prison has been engaged in brutal and inhumane prisoner abuse. The lawyer's railings against the system alone, however, do not really amount to a societal condemnation of the brutality the audience has witnessed. The viewer only feels vindicated when the jury speaks—for the first and only time in the film—and vocalizes the likely reaction shared by the audience that the prison personnel is reprehensible by virtue of their cruel treatment of inmates, driving one to insanity and murder. Similarly, the moment of triumph in *Ghosts of Mississippi* comes when the modern-day jury, almost thirty years after the shooting of civil rights leader Medgar Evers, finally does what two prior hung juries could not: convict the White supremacist Byron De La Beckwith by finding him guilty of murder. The jury gives words, or more accurately the single word of "guilty," to the audience's moral indignation about this racial injustice that had been allowed to persist for over three decades.

Ironically, the voice of the public conscience represented by the jury is silent for the vast majority of the time except for the brief words of the verdict, where indeed, no other voice matters. An analysis of the visuals in *Murder in the First* shows the jury of two women and ten men on screen only once or twice over the course of the trail. The jurors even go unseen when their "not guilty" verdict is read aloud. (This is true also for the unseen reading of the verdict in *A Civil Action*.) But the jury foreman is shown full screen in close-up when he reads a petition from the jury calling for a full investigation of Alcatraz and accusing its wardens of being guilty of "crimes against humanity." Cinematically, this jury is a shadow presence in the court for the vast majority of the film trial until it becomes anything but silent when it articulates the audience's disgust about the prison abuse. Similarly, in *The Rainmaker*, although shots of the jury throughout the trial are more prevalent, the verdict is also delivered by a jury foreman shot from behind until he reads the award for punitive damages ("fifty million dollars"), when he is shown head-on in a predominant medium shot. In *Anatomy of a Murder*, after voir dire the jury is shown only in the background over the shoulders of the lawyers arguing in the case. When the jury is delivering their verdict, however, they enter the courtroom and stand directly facing of the judge, shown in full shot from over the judge's shoulder. In that predominant position, they speak for the first and only time and deliver their verdict of not guilty by reason of insanity. In *The Verdict*, once the jury is impaneled, it is shown only from behind and a few times over the shoulder of the plaintiff's lawyer, Frank Galvin, played by Paul Newman. Even when the jury is shown for the length of Galvin's closing argument it is from behind, so all we see is the impassioned lawyer through the shadowy, out-of-focus figures of the jury. The jurors are shown in full only twice: once when the judge instructs them to ignore a witness's testimony, and then, appropriately for a film called *The Verdict*, head-on as they reenter the courtroom to read their final decision. A similar technique is used in *The Rainmaker*, with two jurors and later a few more acting as out-of-focus bookends in the foreground to the center of the action: the two closing arguments of the lawyers. The jurors are shown head-on, however, when they reenter the courtroom following their deliberations, ready to read their verdict. Likewise in *Jagged Edge*, the jury is shown head-on entering the courtroom to deliver its verdict.

Usually in legal cinema, with the exception of the verdict reading described above, the jury is an almost invisible presence, giving the proceedings legitimacy but never having an identity unto itself. For example, in *Erin Brockovich*, the jury is seen in a far away long shot in the right corner of the screen. Both visually and in terms of lines, the jury very often is only a cinematic presence when its judgment is about to become known. Likewise, in *True Believer*, we never even get to see a verdict from the jury, and the faces of the jurors are rarely shown at any other time during the trial. The jury is first shown from the side and behind, then from above, other times in profile, and once or twice in the distance and even a little out of focus, over the shoulder of an attorney.

Other than at the verdict, the jury might also be given some cinematic presence (albeit usually a silent one) to serve the traditional chorus function of being a mirror in which we can sometimes see a societal reaction to the trial's proceedings. For example, a filmmaker may show a jury member smile knowingly during a witness's testimony, grimacing in reaction to a piece of evidence, or looking away with contempt in response to the simple appearance of a plaintiff or defendant. In moments like these, the filmmaker allows the jury to display a real-time reaction to what is happening in the trial, in many instances reflecting the sentiments of both the jurors and the viewers of the film.

Sometimes the jury reaction is disapproving. In *The Devil's Advocate*, during the trial that opens the film, the jury is shown twice looking with horror and disgust at the defendant, a teacher accused of molesting a student, as his victim testifies as to how the teacher seduced her during school. In *Philadelphia*, the jury is shown squirming in discomfort when it hears of the anonymous sexual encounters that the gay defendant Andrew Beckett sought out in a local porn theater. When Erin Brockovich is a plaintiff and a witness in her case against a driver who ran a red light and severely injured her, we see the jury react disapprovingly when they hear that Erin has two ex-husbands. In *The Rainmaker*, we see two African American women jurors look at each other to register contemptuous disbelief in reaction to a witness's testimony that the crooked insurance company was, "playing odds that the uninsured would not consult a lawyer" when it customarily rejected claims submitted by policyholders. Interestingly, this is really the only time the jury is allowed to show a reaction in the film. Although there are many cutaway shots to the jury that appear to look for a reaction from a juror, none is forthcoming, and they all sit as if intentionally poker faced. Perhaps this is to increase the uncertainty about a verdict for the aggrieved plaintiff and thus the film's dramatic tension, or perhaps it is for the reason that will be discussed later: the filmmakers' desire to preserve the jury's appearance as a truly neutral arbitrator.

Sometimes the jury reaction captured by the filmmakers is shock. The jurors in the trial in *JFK* look away in horror when they are shown the graphic shot of the president's head after being blown apart by a bullet. Similarly, the jurors in *Presumed Innocent*, especially one middle-aged woman shown in close-up, react in horror to pictures of a bloody crime scene. One female juror in *A Time to Kill* is shown with a horrified reaction during the defendant's testimony about his daughter's rape. Later, during the defense's summation, another juror is shown in close up crying through her closed eyes as Matthew McConaughey graphically describes the kidnapping, beating, and rape of the defendant's little daughter. One juror in *Jagged Edge* is shown dabbing her eye after the testimony of a victim describing a horrific attack, where she was tied up in bed by a masked assailant who used a knife to cut around her nipple and write the word "bitch" on the wall in her blood. The jurors in *Philadelphia* must literally look away in disgust when Andrew Beckett is asked on the witness stand to remove his shirt and expose the many lesions that cover his torso.

Sometimes, the jury is allowed to show sympathy with a client or witness. In *A Civil Action*, one juror is shown looking down in sadness and pity and another is seen holding back tears when the jury hears of the suffering that the innocent plaintiffs have suffered at the hands of the corporations that have callously allowed the town's water supply to be poisoned. When an elderly witness is ripped apart by the defense lawyer, played by Mary Elizabeth Mastrantonio, in *Class Action*, the jury turns away from the witness in embarrassment. Like the audience, the jury feels sympathy for this corporate whistle-blower who has been exposed as easily confused and perhaps even senile, forgetting or mixing up numbers, including his own phone number and social security number.

Sometimes we see the jury commiserating without words with one side or the other through their reactions to a witness, to a piece of evidence, or to a lawyer's statement. The jury in *JFK* laughs along with prosecuting lawyer Jim Garrison when he sarcastically jokes about the preposterousness of the government's claim about a ricocheting "magic bullet" that would have had to turn in midair to make the injuries it is purported to have caused. Later on, though, the jury appears to signal that Garrison has gone too far, as a number of jurors shake their heads in disbelief at Garrison's claims of a far-reaching government cover-up. Another jury, in *Ghosts of Mississippi*, is shown laughing with the assistant district attorney's sarcastic comment about why a witness did not come forward with an alibi for his friend until after the friend sat in jail for eight months. In *My Cousin Vinny*, one hometown juror is shown smiling in solidarity with a witness who says, "No self-respecting southerner uses instant grits!" Another actually says quietly, "That's right!" when a witness talks about getting her car stuck in the famous mud of Beechum County, Alabama. The jurors also look at each other and signal their skepticism toward a witness who claims to have identified the defendants past a row of trees and through windows caked with dirt.

In *Trial and Error* (another film directed by *Vinny*'s Jonathan Lynn), the jurors momentarily rally behind the hometown defendant, smiling tenderly at him when he says on the witness stand, "That's why, folks, our town . . . is the warm home I always dreamed of." The jury as a whole, however, goes back and forth from the prosecution to the defense. First, jurors look at each other and giggle when the district attorney tears apart the credibility of the defense's inexperienced and only lightly credentialed "expert" witness. Later, they sit enraptured by the defendant's outlandish story of childhood woe, moving from sympathetic horror (one juror literally has her mouth agape, and another audibly gasps) to pity and sympathy (one male juror weeps and removes his glasses to wipe his eyes, and another struggles to hold back the tears). A middle-aged, White male juror in *A Time to Kill* is shown exchanging smiles with the district attorney prosecuting Carl Lee Hailey, the Black man who murdered his daughter's rapists. One of the jurors in *Philadelphia* laughs in recognition when a witness explains the sexual atmosphere when he was ship board in the Navy by saying, "There were no women in the Navy." The juror then smiles and subtly nods in approval when the witness, a senior partner in the defendant's law firm, tells of how he and his buddies they "taught a lesson" to a gay sailor by, "sticking his head in a latrine after eleven of us had used it."

Sometimes, the jury is simply doing what the audience or what a person who was placed in that jury box would like to do. The exclusively male jurors in *Chicago* all lean in to get a closer look at Roxie Hart when she exposes her leg while testifying on the witness stand. The jurors in *Trial and Error* also lean forward to get a better look at evidence when presented: pennies that were sold fraudulently as "copper engravings of the great emancipator" for $17.99 each. More juror aerobics occur in *The Rainmaker*, with the jury leaning in with rapt attention when the judge overrules a lawyer's objection to his opponent soliciting repetitious testimony, saying, "I want the jury to hear this." The jurors in *Jagged Edge* lean in twice, once eagerly to get a look at a love letter from a witness to the defendant, and again when, like the court and the audience, it waits with anxious anticipation to hear a key answer from a witness about the proper identification of a possible murder weapon. One juror in *The Wrong Man* speaks up for bored jurors everywhere when he literally stands up during a technical, repetitious piece of testimony and says loudly to the judge, "Your honor, do we have to sit here and listen to this?"

In addition to being a chorus that will react to pieces of the trial in front of it and then, in the verdict, speak its judgment (and the judgment of society in a broader sense), the jury in many other ways is a stand-in for the audience. In *Chicago*, lawyer Billy Flynn actually mistakenly refers to the jury as "the audience": It is an easy mistake to make. Similar to the audience, the jurors are passive witnesses to the action of the cinematic trial, powerless to affect what is occurring in front of them. Similar to the audience, once impaneled, the jury must watch the unfolding events and remain mostly still and quiet, whether it approves of the proceedings or not. And yet, both the jury and the audience are supremely powerful, in that in the end, all that will matter is their judgment of what they have witnessed.

Finally, like the movie audience, the jury is the body to which all the proceedings are directed. The judge works hard to protect the integrity of what the jury will hear and see, just as the director controls what the audience will witness and experience. The lawyer pleads his or her case to the jury just as the writer and other filmmakers try to impart their point of view onto the audience. Cinematically speaking, this is sometimes accomplished literally.

As mentioned earlier, Frank Galvin's closing argument in *The Verdict* is delivered through Paul Newman to the camera directly with only a few out-of-focus jurors in the foreground to block the view, as are the closing arguments of both lawyers in *The Rainmaker*. The district attorney's opening statement in *Presumed Innocent* is played into the camera in almost exactly the same way, and evidence is also proffered by the district attorney directly to the jury and audience in close-up. Both the lawyers in *Philadelphia* make their cases directly to the camera, with the camera then cutting to the jury, using montage to make the audience the jury. In an even more blatant example of the filmmakers' speaking to the audience through the jury, director and cowriter Oliver Stone brings the camera in *JFK* directly behind the jury for the final summation of his protagonist, District Attorney Jim Garrison (Kevin Costner). This allows Costner to move his gaze up from the jurors and directly into the camera to utter his final plea, "Do not forget your dying king.... It's up to you." He speaks to the camera through the jury, and thus to the audience and all of America. Similarly, Deputy District Attorney Kathryn Murphy, played by Kelly McGillis, in *The Accused* is directed to speak directly into the camera at the close of her summation by putting the camera (and thus the audience) directly in the jury box. In *Ghosts of Mississippi*, Assistant District Attorney Bobby DeLaughter, played by Alec Baldwin, is held in close-up during his closing argument and delivers the film's core message directly into the camera and to the audience: "Is it ever too late to do the right thing?" he asks, trying to get a conviction against a racially motivated killer three decades after his crime. "For the sake of justice and for the hope of us as a civilized society, I sincerely pray that it is not."

So why is there this unwritten rule in legal cinema that the jury is to be seen but not heard? Why is the jury such a nonentity throughout the history of legal films, when every other legal player has frequent moments in the spotlight? Perhaps it is because filmmakers want to portray the jury as audiences probably like to think of it: a blank slate comprised of completely neutral and fair decision makers. Filmmakers do not let juries speak or even have much of a visible film presence for fear of ruining the illusion of perfect justice. As discussed earlier, although director Francis Ford Coppola cuts to the jurors many times during *The Rainmaker*, even in close-up, almost begging for their reaction to a bit of trial business that has played out in front of them, we are given nothing except for a small look between two jurors at one point. Whether it is realistic for the jury to be so stone-faced when confronted with the jarring testimony and evidence it witnesses is debatable, but it certainly allows the jury to retain its mystique as a perfectly neutral decision-making body that shall not be swayed by emotion nor make any premature judgments before hearing all sides of a case.

The complete anonymity with which the jurors are portrayed in the vast majority of cinematic cases helps perpetuate the idea that the jury is so neutral and fair that it is almost invisible. The jurors with whom we spend over ninety minutes in *Twelve Angry Men* are referred to only by their juror numbers. There is only a brief moment outside the courtroom at the close of the film when elderly Juror #9 introduces himself to the white knight Juror #8, played by Henry Fonda. "What's your name?" the old gent played by Joseph Sweeney asks. "Davis," responds Fonda. "Mine's McCartle." Then there is an awkward pause in which the two men seem to realize that there is nothing more to say because the reason for their interaction was concluded with the delivering of their verdict. "Well, so long," says #9, breaking the silence. "So long," says Fonda with a smile, walking off into world presumably never to see his fellow jurors ever again, or even to know the names of the other ten. The jurors in *Philadelphia* are not even given the dignity of being individuals, even if only identified by number. They are billed in the credits as a group simply as "The Jury."

Sometimes, however, the jury is portrayed as virtually invisible because justice has not been done. The first shot of *Presumed Innocent* is of the courtroom with a slow zoom into the empty jury box. As the camera comes to rest on the twelve empty wooden chairs, the narration by Harrison Ford says, "[The jury] alone must determine what really happened.... If they cannot find the truth, what is our hope of justice?" This is ominous foreshadowing in a movie that will leave the audience guessing until the very end as to who really is guilty of murder. The jury will in fact get it right (sort of) when it finds Rusty not guilty, but the guilty party will go free. Director Alan J. Pakula tacks on an accusatory coda by ending the film with the same shot with which he started: an empty jury box. When the jury is missing, either literally or in failing to find the truth hidden in a trial, justice has left the building.

Runaway Jury also has a symbolic shot of twelve empty chairs in the jury box, which is appropriate for a movie that has one of the characters ask rhetorically, "I mean, is there even such a thing as an objective jury?" The jury in *Primal Fear* is not seen until over an hour and half into the movie, well after the trial has commenced. It is only shown in brief shots after that, mostly over the shoulders of the lawyers. Again, a jury that misreads the truth and mistakenly allows for a miscarriage of justice is made to be invisible in the trial's proceedings. Director Robert Mulligan uses clever camera techniques to keep the jury that will deliver its unjust verdict in *To Kill a Mockingbird* almost faceless. No juror is ever shown in close-up. The jury is shown from above, at a distance, from behind, and in the shadows. Even their verdict is delivered far away and in profile. The only time we get anything approaching a good look at the faces of the jurors is when they are seen over the shoulder of the district attorney as he cross-examines the "negro" suspect Tom Robinson. The members of the jury can almost be mistaken for part of the prosecuting team, a kind of legal lynch mob all ganging up on the innocent defendant.

Sometimes juries in film are visually presented not as absent or derelict in their duties but as less than completely impartial. Like the judge, the jury in *Chicago* is shown in a symbolic musical number as being seduced by the razzle-dazzle of defense lawyer Billy Flynn and his team of voluptuous and scantily clad circus showgirls seated on the laps of the exclusively male jury members. Sex appeal also appears to play a role in affecting the jury in *The Devil's Advocate.* Handsome young lawyer Kevin Lomax, played by Keanu Reeves, plays on his looks, bragging, "I never had a jury without a woman on it." Indeed, the big case at the center of the film ends up with nine female jurors, many of whom are shown in close-up closely watching Kevin in his opening statement. Men are shown too, but not nearly as much. Likewise, Don Johnson as the attractive and seductive client in *Guilty as Sin* goes over and thanks the jurors for their "hopelessly deadlocked" hung verdict. One man and one woman refuse to shake his hand, but two women shake his hand, smiling and looking away coyly.

At least one film raises the possibility that class may be a hindrance to the defendant being fairly judged by the jury. Investigator Sam Ransom, played by Robert Loggia in *Jagged Edge,* questions whether his wealthy client can get a fair shake from the jury: "A rich guy like Forrester," he says, "where the hell is he going to get a trial of his peers? He's gonna get a bunch of people who hate him for what he's got."

Some juries come with the filmmakers' implication that racial differences might make neutrality and impartiality difficult, if not impossible. To a large degree, juries in legal cinema have diversified as the nation has become more diverse, or more accurately, as the relative political power of traditionally disempowered groups has grown. In this way, the jury at the very least is inherently an indirect instrument of the power of the majority, reflecting the political power of groups at the time of trial. The jury in the 1930s trial portrayed in *The Untouchables*, for example, is all White and mostly older men. The 1950s jury in *Twelve Angry Men* is all male (as the title would denote) and all White, whereas the jury in *Anatomy of a Murder* is men and women, but mostly old and all White. The 1960s jury in *JFK* is all male but racially mixed. This is in contrast to the 1980s jury in *Legal Eagles* or the 1990s jury in *My Cousin Vinny*, which are composed of men and woman and are multigenerational and multiracial. The 1990s jury in *The Rainmaker* even has an African American foreperson. The new millennium jury in 2003's *Runaway Jury* takes diversity to a new height. There are female, African American, and Latino jurors. There is also a blind juror—perhaps the first big-screen portrayal of a person with a disability as part of a jury.

For many early legal films, the homogenized jury is less of an indication that biases are at work, at least not so as to significantly affect the outcome of the trial. In other cases, however, the majority makeup of the jury will be crucial, particularly when the defendant is a minority. In *A Time to Kill*, the concern is made explicit. Before jury selection (much less the trial) even begins, characters in the film speak about the trial involving the African American defendant Carl Lee Hailey and say things like, "Pick the right jury and you walk. D.A. picks the jury and you get the gas," and, "Without Blacks on the jury Hailey doesn't have a chance in Hell." When an all-White jury remains after all of the defense's challenges are used up, Carl Lee asks incredulously, "That's a jury of my peers?!" His lawyer, played by Matthew McConaughey, can only respond, "God bless America." The audience is left to ponder whether a Black man who has killed two White men can nonetheless be seen by an all-White jury as being justified (or at least temporarily insane) in avenging the kidnapping, beating, and raping of his ten-year-old daughter.

In *Ghosts of Mississippi*, we see how the institutional racism of the times creates juries that are reflective of majority power and allows jury bias to result in a miscarriage of justice. We never see the juries that were unable to reach a verdict in the first two murder trials of slain civil rights leader Medgar Evers, but those 1960s juries are described many years later by a character as two "all male, all White" juries. By contrast, the jury in the 1994 trial at the center of this film has a minority of White jurors (it is two-thirds people of color, to be precise), is of mixed age, and is composed of both men and women. The jury foreman is even an elderly Black man. This jury has finally reached some racial balance as Mississippi and the nation as a whole have moved away from being so starkly oppressive to African Americans. Not coincidentally, it is also this jury that will finally do justice and bring a guilty verdict against the racist assassin, played by James Woods.

In other films, problems with the racial composition in the jury are more implied. The judge in *The Hurricane* says to the wrongly accused defendant, Rubin "Hurricane" Carter, "Although you still contend you are not guilty of the crimes charged against you, you were afforded a fair trial by a jury of your peers." Immediately after the judge's statement, the film cuts to a shot of the all-White jury. The insult is compounded when the guilty verdict is read aloud by the White jury foreman. The visual juxtaposition of the black defendant in the mid-1960s being found guilty of a triple homicide by an exclusively White jury is both tragic and ironically comic; the viewer must laugh at the cutaway to the all-White jury when the judge utters the phrase, "jury of your peers," but then must shake his head at the hypocritical injustice.

These visual portrayals of the jury as skewed whether by race or other reasons, however, are the exception in legal cinema. Far more often, the jury is shown through its invisibility to be an open repository for testimony and evidence—a kind of sponge for the truth. Because we like to think of the jury as an idealization of pure, fair decision making, it is mostly portrayed in film as an enigma that almost magically creates justice in the form of a verdict. A character in *Anatomy of a Murder* literally refers to it as, "One of the miracles of man's disorganized soul." There is rarely any suspicion of anything occurring between the lawyers' closing arguments and the verdict other than the logical, almost predetermined outcome of the trial. Most times, the verdict seems to be almost nothing more than the continuation of a thought started by the most persuasive lawyer in his or her closing argument. One would almost suspect the juries that arrive at these verdicts are not composed of human beings with their own agendas and biases but of computers that weigh the arguments and the evidence coldly and logically so that justice may prevail.

Only in a handful of cinematic instances is the curtain of mystery that surrounds the jury and its deliberations pulled aside so that we are allowed to see the usually unseen human element that is an inextricable part of every jury verdict. Filmmakers appear as loathe to reveal the secret behind the magic as a magician is to show the wires, mirrors, or trap doors on his favorite trick, for in losing the invisibility of the jury's deliberation, we also lose the pretense that juries are always fair and do little more than reach the forgone conclusion to the drama that has preceded their decision making.

In most cases, we are allowed only a brief glimpse of jury deliberation. In *Ghosts of Mississippi*, our exposure to it is only aural: a shot of the closed jury room door from which we can hear the yelling of the deliberating jurors. In *A Time to Kill*, we are given a more significant insight into the mind of the jury, though in this film we see them before deliberations begin. The jurors are shown a few times at dinner while they are sequestered. Despite the judge's order not to discuss the case until its completion, they secretly take a straw poll about halfway through the trial that shows seven jurors finding the defendant guilty, four undecided, and one voting not guilty. They vote again the night before the lawyers' summary arguments, and all are unanimous in their guilty verdict. This directorial and screenwriting trick is probably used to increase the odds against the defendant, and thus the dramatic stakes for the protagonist lawyer, and to make his accomplishment of securing a verdict of not guilty all the more significant and more exclusively a solo achievement. *Suspect* spends more time with jurors than is customary because one of the film's stars, Dennis Quaid, is a juror. He is anything but invisible, even going to the extreme of investigating witnesses himself in some dangerous situations and tipping off one of the lawyers to a discovery he makes about a piece of evidence. Still, we never get to follow this very visible juror or his colleagues into the jury room.

For that step, we need a movie like *Philadelphia* to invite the audience into the jury room for a brief but significant glimpse into how the jury arrived at its just conclusion. We see and hear the juror who earlier had been shown smiling in solidarity with the witness as he testified about his time in the Navy when he and his buddies "taught a lesson" to a gay sailor on board by assaulting and humiliating him. To our surprise, we now see him in the jury room defending the gay plaintiff played by Tom Hanks and questioning the honesty and motives of the senior partners at the law firm who fired him.

The most serious, memorable, and effective cinematic analysis of the role of the jury in the legal system is undoubtedly *Twelve Angry Men*, the *Citizen Kane* of jury movies. Perhaps the fact that only a handful of films since its release have been dedicated to juries is a testament to its effectiveness: There does not appear to be much more to say on the subject. The film is so significant in the history of legal cinema because it so jarringly runs against the rule we have just discussed. Rather than making the jury's decision nothing more than a validation of the lawyers' arguments, the jury is shown warts and all, for ill as well as good, as a body filled with its own agendas, prejudices, perspectives, and ability to reason. Ironically, those very human traits do not add up to a condemnation of the jury system as one that strays beyond logic and cold facts but, instead, become a testament to the wisdom of having human beings and not something akin to computers judging other human beings in matters involving the human condition.

The film (and the play that inspired it, both wonderfully written by Reginald Rose) is as ingenious as it is simple and efficient. It involves a capital murder trial of a young, poor "slum" kid accused of murdering his father with a switchblade knife. Unlike most legal movies, this one begins where most film trials end. The film opens with the judge charging the jury and sending it off to deliberate. We see the defendant, and then the empty jury room, and only then does the title of the film appear. For the remainder of the film we do not leave that small jury room, except to follow a juror or two into the restroom and for a brief epilogue outside the courtroom at the film's conclusion. Neither do we interact with any character who is not a juror, except a bailiff who sticks his head in when called for or when he hears a scuffle among the jurors. The preliminary vote in the jury room is eleven guilty and one not guilty, with Juror #8, played memorably and powerfully by Henry Fonda, standing alone. The majority of the time is spent watching the jurors hash it out to reach the unanimous verdict required by law.

On the dark side, *Twelve Angry Men* shows the various human jurors as impatient, timid, meek, subject to peer pressure, prejudiced, and weighed down by personal emotional baggage (to use a pop psychology term that did not exist when the film was made in 1957). Jack Warden plays Juror #7, a wisecracking marmalade salesman. He wants out of the jury room as soon as possible to use the tickets he has to a ball game that evening. He cares so much for his time and so little for justice that he changes his vote from guilty to not guilty just to move things along. He is confronted by a juror who supports acquittal but condemns him for playing "with a man's life" and not having "the guts" to stand by his beliefs. As will often be the case for real life juries, the duty of jury service will be seen as an inconvenience to many and can get in the way of true justice being done.

John Fiedler, whose voice is well known as Piglet in the Walt Disney *Winnie the Pooh* cartoons, is an appropriate choice to play the meek Juror #2. A short, mousy bank employee, he initially votes guilty with the rest of the jury but can not articulate why. When the jurors decide to each take a turn expressing the reasoning behind their decision, all he can say is, "I just think he's guilty." Similarly, Robert Webber plays Juror #12, a slick but shallow advertising executive. When he changes his vote to not guilty, he gives an almost embarrassed smirk. Later, when confronted by one of the more vocal proponents for conviction, he momentarily changes his vote back to guilty. At one point he is derided as "bouncing back and forth like a tennis ball" but says nothing to defend himself. Both Jurors #2 and #12 seem to stand for the truism that most people will be easily swayed by the majority or just go along with the crowd to avoid making waves or standing out. This is not necessarily the motivation one likes to think of as driving a verdict that can lead to the death of an accused man.

Prejudice is broadly represented in the film, though interestingly it is not based on race or skin color. The juror representing bigotry is Juror #10, a garage owner played with commitment by Ed Begley. Although the defendant appears definitely to be something other than a White, Anglo-Saxon Protestant (perhaps being of Italian heritage), Begley could just as easily be reacting to the defendant's poverty or his upbringing in the slums as his ethnicity when he says things like, "I've lived among them all my life. You can't believe a word they say, you know that. I mean they're born liars." He eventually alienates the entire jury, and they literally turn away from him one by one as he goes into a bigoted rant, spewing prejudiced statements like, "You know how these people lie.... They get drunk, oh they're real big drinkers, all of them!... By nature. Violent! Human life doesn't mean as much to them as it does to us.... They're no good. There's not a one them who's any good!" He ends up defeated and quarantines himself to a table in the corner of the jury room, where he will remain silent for the rest of the film except to quietly and in a kind of posttraumatic daze change his vote to not guilty. The saintlike Juror #8 is understanding but firm: "It's difficult to keep personal prejudice out of a thing like this. Whenever you run into it, prejudice always obstructs the truth."

Juror #3, the owner of a messenger service played in a masterful and boisterous, but modulated, performance by Lee J. Cobb, stands for the proposition that it is sometimes hard to look past one's own pain and to avoid improperly transferring negative feelings from one's personal life experience onto the defendant in a trial. From the very beginning, Cobb's juror says, "I have no personal feelings, I just want to talk about facts." Ironically, for this juror in particular, nothing could be further from the truth. When he becomes the lone hold out for a guilty verdict, the audience is able to piece together that the juror has been harboring a painful grudge against his twenty-two-year-old-son, who punched his father two years earlier before disappearing from his life. The juror has transferred, probably unintentionally, that grudge onto the young defendant, saying "He's got to burn! You're letting him slip through our fingers!" In the climatic moment of the film, he looks at a picture of himself with his son and says, "Rotten kids!" He rips the picture violently, catches himself in his own self-deception, and then says quietly through his tears, "Not guilty! Not guilty." His inability to forgive his son for an action the father may have helped precipitate clouded his ability to see the facts in this case, spurring him into seeking vengeance on a defendant who has done nothing wrong other than being young, resembling his son, and being accused of hurting his father.

The human tendency to draw on our emotions and our experience as well as our logic is shown to have its positive side, too. The elderly, presumably retired, Juror #9, played by Joseph Sweeney, is able to see himself in the elderly witness who testified that he saw the defendant run out of the building after hearing a body drop to the floor. He suggests that the man was motivated by "attention, maybe" to make "himself believe that he saw the boy" so as to be paid attention to after a life of little consequence. It is an insight that only someone in that juror's position could have, adding an element of truth to the trial that would otherwise be missing if it were left only to the lawyers and other, younger jurors. Juror #5, played by a very youthful Jack Klugman, is the youngest of the jurors and comes from a background similar to that of the defendant. As a result, he is able to explain the faulty accusation that the boy used a switchblade knife to stab his father in a downward angle. Because he had seen his share of knife fights (unlike any other juror), he knew how to use the weapon—in an upward, jabbing angle—and that the defendant, who had previously been arrested for knife fighting, would know how to use it too. Again, it is an insight that could only come with someone with that particular life experience and that would be likely to be overlooked by the lawyers.

Empathy is considered a virtue in the jury room of *Twelve Angry Men*, and no one personifies the trait more than Juror #8—the feeling, skeptical architect and father of three, played by Henry Fonda in one of his greatest screen performances. Dressed in a white suit, Fonda is lit early on so that his eyes are more pronounced than the rest of his face, visually implying that only he can see the truth. He is smart, convincing, reasonable, and even-tempered, and most of all he feels for the boy on trial. He starts not by saying that the accused boy is innocent but that he "doesn't know" whether he is or not. The juror does think that the others owe the boy some time and thought and that they should not just quickly send him to his death with a guilty verdict. Juror #8 often says what he would do "if it were me" in the defendant's chair. It is his sympathy, or even perhaps pity, that motivates him to take a stand and force the rest of the jury to actually deliberate instead of acting on superficial appearances, gut reactions, or worse, the suspect motivations discussed above.

Above all, the jurors bring a respect for reason and fairness to their deliberations. Facts and intellect trump anything else and are the only weapons that silence the more vociferous jurors who are acting from a place of less lofty ideals. Logic is even used to make up for any inadequacies of the lawyers. Henry Fonda as Juror #8 points out that that the court-appointed attorney was not very good, possibly because the young lawyer resented being put on a case that seemed like a loser from the start. "What kind of bum is he?" one of the jurors asks, referring to the defendant's lawyer. "That's just what I've been trying to find out," Fonda replies. To compensate for what many in the jury room suspect was a weak defense, entire sections of the trial are basically retried in the jury room. The jurors repeatedly ask to reexamine exhibits such as the murder weapon and a diagram of the apartment where the murder occurred. In one memorable sequence, Henry Fonda as Juror #8 reenacts whether the elderly witness who walked with a limp could make it from his bed to the front door in the amount of time he would need to properly identify the killer.

But even facts and reason are shown to be a blindfold if not tempered with analysis, insight, instinct, and life experience. The character of Juror #4, a stockbroker played by E. G. Marshall, represents pure logic, and he is the second-to-last holdout for a guilty verdict. He is not motivated by any personal agenda or improper motivation; he simply has weighed the facts as presented and come to a logical, almost unshakable conclusion. His sin is his unwillingness to delve deeper, to analyze, and to weigh the credibility of the witnesses presented at trial. He takes the data presented to him at face value, just as a stockbroker of the time (pre-Enron) might be prone to do. It is only when the other jurors cast doubt on the testimony as presented that he begins to waver. The scales are tilted when he removes his glasses, the symbolic representation of his intellectualism. Another juror (the elderly Juror #9, cementing his status as probably the most observant juror) points out the small indentations on either side of Juror #3's nose, where his glasses were resting. Juror #9 mentions that they were also present on nose of the female witnesses who claims to have seen the murder from inside her apartment while lying in bed from some distance away. Marshall's juror is then convinced that she was not wearing glasses when witnessing the murder and thus could not really identify the culprit. It is only when he takes off his glasses—the tool that normally allows him to see what is real—that he is able to look past his cold, hard, supposed "facts" and see the truth.

The other jurors are good, decent men but are unlikely to think too hard for themselves, especially when the vast bulk of opinion is going the other way. The foreman, Juror #1, played by Martin Balsam, is an assistant high school football coach who is presumably used to taking direction from the head coach. Juror #11, played by George Voskovec, is a watchmaker and a European immigrant with shaky English, who appears at first a little timid about asserting his doubts, possibly because of his status as a new citizen. Finally, Juror #6, played by Edward Binns and appropriately acting as the middleman, is a self-described "working man"—a house painter. He is perfectly satisfied to be deliberating the case and acts as a counterweight to the impatience of Warden's Juror #7. "Beats working," he says. He admits to taking things at face value, saying, "My boss usually does the supposing." He says sarcastically to Fonda's Juror #8 while the two are in the restroom after a little bit of a row between the others, "Nice bunch of guys, huh?" "Oh, they're about the same as anyone else," Fonda replies. This, of course, is the point of the whole movie.

This observation about the humanity of the jury and how it affects the outcome of a trial is given a much more cynical spin in *Runaway Jury*, probably the film after *Twelve Angry Men* to most deeply delve into the functioning of a jury. The subject of this movie, however, is how the human element makes juries not stronger but weaker and more easily manipulated.

The gimmick of *Runaway Jury* is to focus on jury consultants, those people paid large sums of money not to litigate a case but exclusively to select a sympathetic jury. In *Runaway Jury*, the nation's premiere jury consultant, played with wonderful cynicism by Gene Hackman, is Rankin Fitch, another character with a name straight out of Dickens, apparently a trademark of novelist John Grisham, who wrote the book on which the film is based. Fitch is not only a jury selector but is also a jury tamperer. He is not at all above blackmailing jurors to get the verdict for which his clients have paid. There is a wrench in the works, however: Nick Easter, played by John Cusack, a law student who has had the idealistic wind knocked out of him and who now is a kind of jury con man who manipulates the jury from the inside as a juror himself and then sells the verdict to the highest bidder. Or so it appears.

Runaway Jury is almost a mirror image of *Twelve Angry Men* in terms of faith in the jury system. "Trials are too important to be left to juries," one character says. The jurors are portrayed as being equally flawed as the characters in *Twelve Angry Men*: one has a drinking problem, another is having an affair, one is secretly HIV positive, and another has had a secret abortion. However, these frailties are not used as they are in *Twelve Angry Men* to inform the life experiences of the jurors and give them insight into their deliberations. In this movie, their human condition is a weakness to be preyed on by those seeking to win the case at any cost. Gene Hackman, in his historic scene with costar Dustin Hoffman (a first together for the screen legends and former roommates), asks Hoffman sarcastically, "You think your average juror is King Solomon? No, he's a roofer with a mortgage. He wants to go home and sit in his Barcalounger and let the cable TV wash over him. This man doesn't give a single, solitary droplet of shit about truth, justice, and your American way." In an exchange that serves as a twisted reflection of the conversation between the jurors in *Twelve Angry Men*, Dustin Hoffman, as lawyer Wendell Rohr, says to the jury consultant, "They're people, Fitch," to which Fitch replies, "My point exactly." In *Twelve Angry Men*, the humanity they discuss was a virtue; in *Runaway Jury*, it is a vulnerability.

Though a lesser caliber of film than *Runaway Jury* and a far lesser film than *Twelve Angry Men, The Juror* is another film that goes beyond the normal invisibility of the jury process and gives the audience an intimate look at the functioning of a jury. Like *Runaway Jury*, it is a portrait of a tainted jury. The credit sequence opening the film is a shot of a mural of justice interrupted by passing shadows. In this case, those shadows are cast by mobsters who have threatened the life of a juror—single-mom Annie Laird, played by Demi Moore, and her son—if she does not move the jury to a verdict of not guilty. Again, as in *Runaway Jury*, the jury is shown to be easily manipulated by its human weaknesses. Annie, motivated by legitimate fear and the desire to protect her child, is able to one by one move the jurors off their guilty votes. With one she uses her sexuality, playing on his attraction to her by leading him on and agreeing to a date after the trial is over. With an elderly black woman who says she fears for the safety of her grandchildren if she lets this mobster go free, Annie uses her status as a mother to say, "If you twist the law even just a little for the best of reasons, then the law loses whatever power it's got, and then my child is in more danger than before, and so are your grandchildren." Other jurors argue about matters of race and ethnicity, with the jury forewoman saying to another juror, "I really don't care for the term 'greaseball!'" In the end Annie accomplishes the impossible and turns every juror to a vote of not guilty. She is the metaphorical Juror #8 of this trial, although her actions are not to further justice but for a dark purpose of which the other more gullible jurors are unaware.

One other film must be mentioned as a legal cinema entry that delves into the inner working of the jury: the cinematic classic *Jury Duty*. Surfer dude comedian Pauly Shore plays the Henry Fonda role as the juror who must convince all the other jurors who want to vote guilty into changing their votes. The fact that he is prolonging the deliberations so that he can stay sequestered and avoid being homeless, plus get the standard five dollars a day, should tell anyone all they need to know about this film's cinematic pedigree. The only thing interesting about the film is its attempt to be a blatant comic homage to *Twelve Angry Men*. Just like the classic it is attempting to tribute, the film has the new immigrant juror and the juror with basketball tickets who wants the deliberations to be over in a hurry. The jury starts reenacting events from the trial, such as seeing whether someone the size of the defendant could lift the body he was accused of murdering and then moving it. The Pauly Shore character even watches *Twelve Angry Men* in his hotel room and uses lines from it to convince another juror to change her vote. In addition to these moments of imitation, *Jury Duty* also shares *Twelve Angry Men*'s faith in the jury system. What begins as a cynical attempt by Shore to manipulate the jury for his own selfish purposes actually becomes a quest for the truth and results in the jury going beyond its stereotypes and preconceptions and reaching the right conclusion to set an innocent defendant free. If only the film could have conveyed its noble sentiments while achieving its primary goal of being funny.

In addition to the few films that show a detailed picture of the jury deliberation process and thus deflate its mystique, numerous other films allow for the biases and other human weaknesses of jurors to show through by giving a glimpse of the voir dire process—the process of questioning and selecting jurors for a trial. In *Adam's Rib*, we see one potential juror exposed as a sexist during the voir dire. In *The Devil's Advocate*, the jurors do not really say anything to show their biases, but jury expert Kevin Lomax is able to give the lawyers complete psychological profiles of them during voir dire, based on observation and instinct. All the jurors being questioned in *Inherit the Wind* are on a first-name basis with the bailiff, and Spencer Tracy's Henry Drummond is shown dismissing a few who are too religious to his liking to be fair in a case involving a violation of the law on teaching evolution over creationism. An older female juror being questioned in *My Cousin Vinny* becomes acceptable to the prosecution when she states that it should be left up to families of murder victims to decide the punishment of the defendants—establishing the doubt early on whether Vinny will be able to get a fair jury for his two Yankee defendants in this small, southern town. One potential juror in *The Rainmaker*, played in a cameo by country singer Randy Travis, shows his violent side when he leaps from the jury box and attacks the lawyer who accuses him of lying about having contact with the plaintiff's counsel. A number of other films, including *Trial and Error*, *The Verdict*, and *Anatomy of a Murder*, also show at least some jury selection.

Because of our assertion that filmmakers tend to want to hide the human element that is inherently part of jury deliberations out of a desire to cover the warts of the process, we should probably be surprised at the prevalence of cinematic voir dire, which appears more frequently than films showing jury deliberations. Because the showing of the voir dire process also demystifies the "magic" of the jury by making the imperfections of the jurors more transparent, why aren't filmmakers equally reluctant to expose audience to this phase of the trial? Possibly filmmakers feel like they are on more solid ground by showing potential jurors as human or biased before they actually become jurors. The assumption may be that of course jurors are flawed mortals when they arrive at a courthouse for jury duty. When they transform from citizen to juror, however, they should then be shown as somehow having been unburdened of their everyday preconceptions and biases. Not only does this process allow the filmmaker to preserve the mystique and idealization of the jury but it also allows the myth of the invisible, impartial jury to be reinforced and supplemented. It allows society to feel smug that its citizens understand the solemn duty of being a juror and are able to rise to their higher selves when participating in the legal process to arrive at a verdict.

This theory may also account for why the only films that ever show citizens being reluctant about becoming jurors are the same ones that show the warts-and-all jury process from beginning to end. In general, only films that are striving to show a more intimate, inside view of the jury are comfortable giving cinematic representations of a societal truism: For most Americans, jury duty is seen as an inconvenience and something to get out of. In *Runaway Jury*, John Cusack's Nick Easter describes jury duty by saying, "It's like going to the dentist. It's worse than going to the dentist!" He even admits to "trying to pray my way out of jury duty." In *Suspect*, when Dennis Quaid, as lobbyist Eddie Sanger, is called a second time for jury duty, he still hopes to be excused from having to serve. When he cannot get out of it, a colleague cynically says, "What are you? An immigrant? Nobody has jury duty. Next you're going to tell me you vote!" In *Jury Duty*, one potential juror is shown literally bandaging his head on the courthouse steps in an attempt to get out of having to serve on a jury. At the start of the trial, a long dolly shot shows all the jurors very unhappy about the prospect of a long trial and being sequestered for the length of it. As the judge describes it, "It will be a true test of your commitment of our judicial system." This play to civic duty seems to do little to boost their morale. Throughout the history of legal cinema, only the title character in *The Juror*, Demi Moore's Annie Laird, is shown as actually wanting jury duty. After giving her opportunities to be excused from the jury because of her duties as a single mom, the judge asks her point blank, "So you would like to serve?" "Yes," she replies, "Yes I would." Later on, she explains, "It's a little exciting. I need a little excitement!" As previously discussed, all four of these films have already committed to piercing the veil of secrecy and mystique surrounding the jury. It makes sense they are the only ones willing to show the reluctance of most people to become jurors in the first place. Somehow the triumphant reading of the verdicts in films like *The Rainmaker, A Time to Kill, Ghosts of Mississippi, Murder in the First, Philadelphia,* and *The Verdict* would seem somewhat diminished if the audience had lingering visions of how badly these jurors wanted to be somewhere—anywhere—else rather than sitting on these juries in the first place.

Many films in legal cinema, however, allude to the importance of the jury in creating a fair legal system. As described previously, the opening narration in *Presumed Innocent* refers to the juries as "our hope for justice." When the jury pool enters the courtroom in *Runaway Jury,* they walk in under a door inscribed with the statement "It is the spirit and not the form of the law that keeps justice alive," as if to imply that as long as juries stay true to finding truth, our justice system will prevail. (Of course, the movie is a kind of cautionary tale to what happens when that spirit is manipulated and corrupted.) For all the maneuverings of the lawyers in *A Civil Action,* lawyer Jerry Facher, played by Robert Duvall, puts the trial correctly in context when he tells opposing counsel Jan Schlichtmann, "It's going to come down to people, like it always does." In *The Verdict,* Paul Newman's Frank Galvin accurately tells the jury, "Today you are the law."

For all its importance, the jury remains one of the least explored aspects of the trial process in legal cinema. Ironically, this is not an attempt to dismiss its centrality to the proper functioning of the legal system. To the contrary, it is out of respect for the jury's mystique. It seems the jury has been relegated to being an extra in legal cinema, or at least a bit player, but in actuality it constitutes a character unto itself, whose mere silent presence seems a necessity for the portrayal of a just legal system.

4

Shysters and Saints: The Lawyer

"You're an attorney. Be proud! Your job is to find justice no matter how well she may hide herself from you."
—Donald Sutherland as Lucien Wilbanks in *A Time to Kill*

"Everybody loves lawyer jokes, especially lawyers. They're even sort of proud of them. Why do you suppose that is?"
—Matt Damon as Rudy Baylor in *The Rainmaker*

Have you heard the one about what the difference is between a lawyer and a bucket of pond scum? The bucket. Or what's the difference between a dead skunk in the road and a dead lawyer in the road? There are skid marks in front of the skunk. How about, you are stranded on a desert island with Hitler, Attila the Hun, and a lawyer, but you have a gun with only two bullets. What do you do? Shoot the lawyer twice. One more: What do you have when a lawyer is buried up to his neck in sand? Not enough sand. Everyone knows at least one lawyer joke portraying lawyers as vile, loathsome, dishonest, unprincipled, ruthless, or arrogant. Poll after poll confirms the public's low opinion of lawyers. A 2002 Harris

Poll found that only 24 percent of respondents said they would trust lawyers, whereas 66 percent said they would not. Lawyers even received a lower trustworthy rating in the poll than trade union leaders and members of Congress.[7] A 2003 survey by the American Bar Association found lawyers to be in one of the least reputable professions in the nation, with only the media ranking lower.[8]

Legal cinema knows this public perception of lawyers and often plays off of it. Sometimes, the filmmakers use the public's dislike for lawyers for comic effect, creating a sort of visual lawyer joke. Jeff Daniels as Charles Tuttle in *Trial and Error* steps in and tries to keep two patrons from fighting, but he starts a bar fight when he is asked by one of them, "Are you a lawyer?" and he replies, "Yes." The retort is a punch in the kisser. When the Lost Boys in *Hook* accuse the grown up Peter Pan of being a pirate, he defends himself by saying he is a lawyer. Their response? "Kill the lawyer!" Don Johnson as the client from hell, David Greenhill, in *Guilty as Sin*, says to a friend, "People like us, we're warm people. But she's . . . an attorney!" In *Legally Blonde*, the father of Elle Woods (Reese Witherspoon) tells his daughter, "Oh, sweetheart, you don't need law school. Law school is for people who are boring, ugly and serious." Later when a client asks whether her lawyer boss is always such an ass, one of the other lawyers says, "He's the top defense attorney in the state. Of course he's an ass!" Matt Damon as lawyer Rudy Baylor says in a voice-over in *The Rainmaker*, "Sworn in by a fool and vouched for by a scoundrel, I'm a lawyer at last!" In *Regarding Henry*, the revelers at a cocktail party are discussing how tragic it is that a head injury has caused a successful lawyer to lose his memory and be reduced to the intelligence of a young child. "One minute you're an attorney, the next you're an imbecile," one says. Another quips, "That's not a very long trip." Mobster Tommie Morolto, played by Paul Sorvino in an uncredited role in *The Firm*, tells his goombah colleague, "I swear to you, Joey, every fucking lawyer on the face of the earth ought to be killed." When the Mafia finds lawyers to be lowlife, the legal profession is in real trouble.

Sometimes the prejudice against lawyers is used by filmmakers as a kind of shorthand to quickly paint a character as a person of low morality. In *Regarding Henry*, Harrison Ford's Henry Turner is first shown as a successful but ruthless corporate lawyer. He is unfeeling and materialistic—the sort of person who calls his interior decorator while waiting for a verdict to yell about the gaudiness of a dining room table. He is unreasonably demanding of his young daughter, yelling at her for accidentally spilling grape juice on his piano. It takes a bullet to the head and a coma to transform Henry into a loving, caring human being. On returning home from the rehabilitation clinic, he comments, "nice table" about the same piece of furniture he was yelling about earlier in the film. When his daughter spills juice now and is worried her father will yell at her, he says instead, "That's OK, I do it all the time" and demonstrates by intentionally knocking over his own juice glass with a smile. Henry summarizes his horror at his past cruelty and dishonesty by saying, "I thought I could go back to my life. But I don't like who I was." His maid concurs, "I like you much better now." The filmmakers use Henry's status as a lawyer before he is attacked to quickly establish him as a person in need of redemption: He was an evil lawyer and now he is a lover of puppies.

Strangely, these negative portrayals of lawyers, reflecting the commonly held belief that lawyers, by and large, are of low moral character, are the exception rather than the rule in legal cinema. Although it is true that lawyers are almost always portrayed as being competitive to the point of ruthlessness, confident to the point of being arrogant, and workaholic to the point of being obsessed, they are also presented as passionate, committed, intelligent, and articulate lovers of the law. True, lawyers are shown as being dishonest more than honest, but usually it is in some kind of context. Often the dishonesty is a kind of trickery done in defense of innocent clients who have the system skewed against them or is shown as part of a continuum in which the lawyer moves from a less moral to a more moral center in his or her journey through the film. At the very least, for every morally contemptible lawyer there is often a lawyer with integrity on the other side of the case. In short, lawyers appear to be more often portrayed in legal cinema as we would like to think of them rather than as we actually think of them.

On one point both filmmakers who hold a positive and negative view of lawyers appear to agree: There is no such thing as a lazy lawyer. All lawyers, whether idealistic, cynical, or criminal, are portrayed in legal cinema as being very busy plying their craft, whether for good or ill. District Attorney Kathryn Murphy in *The Accused*, played by Kelly McGillis, is shown working in her office literally until dawn researching to try and find precedent for a claim to hold the spectators of a gang rape as co-conspirators in the crime. Mary Elizabeth Mastrantonio, as corporate lawyer Maggie Ward in *Class Action*, is also shown spending the night in her office. Defense lawyer Eddie Dodd (James Woods) and his young associate Roger Baron (Robert Downey Jr.) are shown in *True Believer* working until dawn going through boxes of old police files and evidence. Eddie is dogged in working for his clients, even to the point of pursuing a prosecutor into the men's room and haranguing him for a plea bargain while the man urinates; Eddie succeeds in getting the reduced sentence he was seeking. Both Tom Hanks's and Denzel Washington's lawyer characters in *Philadelphia* are shown still working at 10:15 at night. In *Anatomy of a Murder*, Jimmy Stewart's Paul Biegler and his friend and ad hoc legal partner Parnell McCarthy (Arthur O'Connell) get literally elbow-deep in law books in an attempt to find a case that will allow them to create a defense for their client based on an uncontrollable urge constituting legal insanity. District Attorney Jim Garrison, played by Kevin Costner in *JFK*, tirelessly pours over the 27 volumes of transcripts of the Warren Commission until late into the evening. Ron Silver, as real-life attorney Alan Dershowitz, has a team of lawyers and law students working in his house on the Claus von Bülow case around the clock like a kind of legal commune in *Reversal of Fortune*. And the movie ... *And Justice for All* has a lot of bad things to say about the legal system, but accusing lawyers of being slackers is not one of them. To the contrary, lawyers in this film are almost held harmless—victims of a system that is stretched too thin, demanding them to do too much and to be in too many places at the same time. The film's protagonist, Arthur Kirkland, played by Al Pacino, is not only being run ragged by his half a dozen clients but also manages to visit weekly the ailing grandfather who raised him. Similarly, Glenn Close's Teddy Barnes in *Jagged Edge* is able to be both a successful lawyer and a loving single mother to her two young children.

Many lawyers are shown as habitually and even unhealthily working on a nonstop basis. When Rebecca De Mornay, as Jennifer

Haines in *Guilty as Sin*, goes to her office after regular hours, she is the only one in the building except for the night security guard, who has seen her so often he knows her by name: "How are you, Ms. Haynes?" She and her lawyer boyfriend complain to each other of never being at home and joke about selling the house because of disuse. She even appears ready to cancel vacations whenever a case warrants it; one partner in the firm says, "We're glad you are not taking that vacation." Cher's Kathleen Riley in *Suspect* is a public defender who does not date, has not been on vacation, and has not even been to a movie in a year. At one point, she says with exasperation to a colleague, "I'm tired, I'm really tired.... I spend all my time with murderers and rapists and what's really crazy is I like them!" When lawyer Rudy Baylor in *The Rainmaker* is awakened from his slumber over a set of law books by a phone call from colleague Deck Shifflet, Baylor asks, "Don't you ever sleep?" After their conversation about a lucky turn of events in the case, they agree to rendezvous and continue working on the case into the night over a fresh supply of coffee. Eddie Dodd in *True Believer* has his bedroom off of his office so that his work is almost literally his life, with only a door separating him from his job. The lawyer, played by Anthony Quayle in *The Wrong Man*, comes to the police station late at night on a moment's notice when the right man—the real criminal who has been robbing neighborhood businesses—is caught, thus clearing his client. One is left to wonder, does this guy not have a life, so he is willing to show up on his own time just to congratulate his client when it could easily wait until the next morning? When the title character in *Regarding Henry* is forced by his head trauma to ask his maid what he used to do before the accident when he was home, the maid replies, "You're working all the time." He presses further, asking, "What am I doing when I'm not working?" At a loss, she says, "You are always working."

Some lawyers are shown in legal cinema as working hard even on the process of becoming a lawyer. As law student Darby Shaw in *The Pelican Brief*, Julia Roberts is shown through a time lapse montage tenaciously working for a week straight in her school's law library, doing research for a legal project. We hear that the title character in *My Cousin Vinny*, Vincent Laguardia Gambini, played so memorably by Joe Pesci, worked at his father-in-law's garage to put himself through the Brooklyn Academy of Law, a school no doubt based on the real-life Brooklyn Law School, which is known for creating tough first-generation lawyers thanks to its evening program. Similarly, lawyer Mitchell McDeere, played by Tom Cruise in *The Firm*, works his way through law school by tending bar. Ditto for Matt Damon's character in *The Rainmaker*. We find out that Susan Sarandon's Reggie Love in *The Client* put herself through law school after the husband she worked to put through medical school left her for a younger woman. Even Elle Woods, played by Reese Witherspoon in *Legally Blonde*, works incredibly hard studying for the LSAT's—even passing up a keg party!

A number of legal films take pains to point out how the workaholic, sometimes obsessive work ethic of lawyers can cost them the love of the ones they hold dear. When Tom Cruise, as lawyer Mitchell McDeere in *The Firm*, continually comes home from work at all hours, constantly missing dinner, his wife begins to get resentful, leaving him a note on the dog suggesting that they eat kibble together. In *Hook*, Robin Williams as lawyer Peter Banning, the grown up Peter Pan, says to his son, "My word is my bond," but he breaks his promise to be at his son's Little League game, and instead sends an office worker to videotape it. His wife later confronts him, saying, "How many more broken promises, Peter?" An ex-lover of attorney Alan Dershowitz (Ron Silver) in *Reversal of Fortune*, played by Annabella Sciorra, tells him, "You give everything you have to the law and you forget the people you care about." He yells back, "My clients are the people I care about!" And even though she is not technically a lawyer, Julia Roberts, as title character *Erin Brockovich*, is a paralegal who becomes as dedicated to her case as any lawyer. Tensions rise with her boyfriend and her children because of how much her case keeps her away from them. She misses the first word spoken by one of her children because she is off working on the case. She sobs while driving in her car when hearing the news. Eventually her boyfriend forces her to choose between the job and him, and she sticks with the case. It all creates the justification for her famous line, when she disclaims any emotional distance from the case that has become her life: "That is my work, my sweat, my time away from my kids! If that's not personal, I don't know what it is!"

Lawyers are often shown to be passionate and committed to their case, their client, or their cause, even to the point of putting their well-being at risk. Sometimes, it is their financial security that is at stake. District Attorney Jim Garrison uses $6,000 worth of funds from his own National Guard savings account to pay for the investigations into the JFK assassination rather than use the public's tax dollars. "This isn't about our two cars," he tells his wife. "Sometimes telling the truth is hard." The lawyer played by Alec Baldwin in *Ghosts of Mississippi* has his truck vandalized when someone spray paints "traitor" on it. District Attorney Jim Trotter in *My Cousin Vinny*, played in a charming and even-handed performance by Lane Smith, tells Vinny that he left a private practice that was making a lot of money and became a prosecutor because of a crisis of conscience about defending guilty clients. Defense lawyer Frank O'Connor in *The Wrong Man*, responds to his potential client who expresses money concerns, "Let's not think about that. Let's concentrate on winning the case. If we can do that, then the rest will take care of itself." Lawyer Fred Gailey, played by John Payne in the original *Miracle on 34th Street*, resigns from his law firm after the partners pressure him to drop the "ridiculous" case of defending Kris Kringle in a sanity hearing. "I can't let Kris down," he tells the woman he has been courting (Maureen O'Hara), "He needs me." When she gets nervous about their financial future together and asks him what kind of cases he could possibly get on his own after leaving the prestigious firm he says, "Probably a lot of people like Kris who are getting pushed around. That's the only fun in law anyway." When she complains that lawyers do not get ahead that way, he says skeptically, "That all depends on what you mean by 'get ahead.'"

Some lawyers risk losing their law practices because of the financial cost of doing the right thing for their client. Lawyer Ed Masry, played wonderfully by Albert Finney in *Erin Brockovich*, has spent years building a small law firm from nothing. Still, he puts it all at risk by taking an expensive toxic tort case with no money up front that will leave him broke if he loses. Matthew McConaughey as Jake Brigance in *A Time to Kill* takes $10,000 for what he estimates would be a $50,000 case and continues trying it even though it becomes clear his client will not be able to raise more than $900. To compound the financial difficulty, the lawyer begins ignoring his other clients because of his obsession with defending a Black man who has killed two White men who raped the client's young daughter. The lawyer in *A Civil Action*, Jan Schlichtmann, played by John Travolta, starts as a cynic, but he and the rest of the lawyers in his firm end up financing the case against corporate wrongdoers by using credit cards, cashing in retirement plans, and putting up the deeds of their homes as collateral on loans. He could have settled the case to pay off the debts, but Schlichtmann says, referring to the clients who have suffered bodily harm and in some cases death or the death of their children, "I owe the families more." Similarly, Paul Newman in his deservedly Oscar-nominated role as Frank Galvin in *The Verdict* is in desperate need of the money from a medical malpractice case. He has had only four cases in three years, and all of them were losers, but when he sees the young woman who has been put in a coma because of the negligence of her doctors, he gives up his $70,000 from a $210,000 settlement, saying to the defendant, "I came here to take your money.... I can't do it. I can't take it. Because if I take the money I'm lost." His friend and former law professor, played by Jack Warden, scolds him, saying, "When they give you the money that means you won!" Frank doesn't agree. "They killed her," he says of the hospital, "Tried to buy it." "That's the fucking point, dummy," Warden's character says to no avail.

Even lawyers who do not stand to suffer financial ruin can nonetheless be shown as generous and giving. Erin Brockovich's boss, Ed Masry, advances her paycheck out of his own pocket shortly after hiring her. He gives her a truck and money for a nanny in the middle of the case. After the case is settled, he gives her a two million dollar bonus. In *The Hurricane*, the two lawyers of Rubin "Hurricane" Carter represented the champion boxer for nineteen years totally pro bono. The new, idealistic law school graduate portrayed by Robert Downey Jr. in *True Believer* is not even getting paid for his seemingly round-the-clock work for his idol, defense lawyer Eddie Dodd, on their case to free an innocent convict. Atticus Finch in *To Kill a Mockingbird* is willing to accept hickory nuts and collard greens as payment for legal work on behalf of a poor farmer. James Stewart as Ransom Stoddard is the attorney who comes to town in *The Man Who Shot Liberty Valence.* He volunteers to teach an illiterate woman to read and ends up putting together a whole class of adults and children, including Mexican children whom he teaches to read in English.

Other times, lawyers put their very careers as attorneys in jeopardy to do right by their client. Kelly McGillis's prosecutor in *The Accused* attacks her boss when he forbids her to go after the men who cheered on the gang of rapists who brutalized Sarah Tobias, played by Jodie Foster. "We owe her. I owe her," she entreats. When he still refuses, she threatens to sue the office, saying defiantly, "I am going to try this case and you're not going to stop me!" Laura Linney, as prosecutor Janet Venable in *Primal Fear,* loses her job when she defies her boss to get a conviction. Despite her boss's desire to protect the Catholic Church from scandal, Linney brings in evidence of sexual abuse by the archbishop. Christian Slater, as James Stamphill in *Murder in the First,* gets fired from his first lawyer job as a public defender when he goes against the direction of his boss and works too hard for his client, Henry—even to the point of suing Alcatraz prison itself. Lawyer Reggie Love (Susan Sarandon) in *The Client* takes the case of eleven-year-old Mark Sway even though he cannot pay her any money. Later, she risks being disbarred or arrested for helping her client recover the body of a dead politician who has been murdered by the mob. She later goes even further than that, risking bodily harm when the mob shows up to kill her young client and anyone else who gets in their way. She does not turn tail and run but stays with Mark and helps him see it through.

Like Reggie, other lawyers in legal cinema are shown going further than risking simply their livelihoods and actually putting themselves in some degree of danger in pursuit of a case. In *Suspect,* the public defender, played by Cher, puts herself in jeopardy by agreeing to meet a witness whom she knows is potentially dangerous. At another point, she goes to a parking lot in a driving rainstorm to break into the victim's abandoned car to get some clues that could exonerate her client. She does all of this for a client who assaults her when she has her first interview with him. Even after that incident, she risks further harm by loosening his hand restraints when he requests it. Lawyer Marty Vail, played by

Richard Gere in *Primal Fear,* is part lawyer and part private investigator, literally chasing down potentially violent witnesses to flesh out his client's story. James Stamphill, in *Murder in the First,* goes to see a potential witness and gets roughed up by a hired thug who has come to intimidate the witness and keep him from testifying. Eddie Dodd in the aptly named *True Believer* actually puts his life on the line when—at gunpoint—he refuses to say that he will keep quiet about the police cover-up that has sent his innocent client to jail for eight years. This is a culmination of his having been ambushed, brutally beaten up, and threatened with death earlier in the film if he took his client's case all the way to trial. Eddie and his young associate, Roger Baron, also put themselves in danger by going to the home of a neo-Nazi to get information on a potential witness. "I can't believe that we're going to see a bunch of Nazis," Roger says. "At night!"

Some lawyers go beyond putting just themselves at risk and have to deal with their families being in the line of fire as the result of the lawyer's commitment to a controversial case. This phenomenon appears frequently enough in legal films to almost become a cliché. Alec Baldwin as Assistant District Attorney Bobby DeLaughter in *Ghosts of Mississippi* must rush his family from his house in the middle of the night when he receives a false bomb threat. He eventually loses his wife because of the harassment and scorn he and his family receive for his prosecution of a White supremacist murderer. DeLaughter raises his kids on his own and must alone comfort his son when he gets beaten up in school and called a "nigger lover." Similarly, Jake Brigance in *A Time to Kill* has his life threatened when he defends a Black man who has killed two White good-old boys. The Ku Klux Klan burns a cross on his lawn, and his daughter is taunted as a "nigger lover." There are attempts to blow up his house that eventually succeed, as his house is burnt to the ground the night before the trial is to begin. The paralegal title character in *Erin Brockovich* has her family threatened by an anonymous phone call presumably from someone connected with the powerful utility interests she and her lawyer boss are taking on. District Attorney Jim Garrison in *JFK* also has his family threatened, presumably by the conspirators involved in the president's assassination. The assaults on his reputation and his dedication (some would say obsession) with the case also cause strife between him and his wife, played by Sissy Spacek. In the end, he is willing to sacrifice the family he loves so much in his search for the truth. This is not a negative portrayal of a lawyer.

Lawyers are shown to be brave in other ways, too. In *Legal Eagles*, Robert Redford as Assistant District Attorney Tom Logan chases an armed murder suspect into a burning building to apprehend the guilty party and clear his accused defendant, played by Daryl Hannah. Gregory Peck as lawyer Sam Bowden in the original *Cape Fear* got involved with the evil Max Cady (Robert Mitchum) when he came upon him in a parking lot one night attacking a young woman. He heard a scuffle, fought off Cady, and then testified against him at his trial. In getting involved in this potentially dangerous situation as the result of a chance encounter, to protect a woman with whom he had no connection, Sam proves himself to be a hero of sorts. Gregory Peck (again) as lawyer Atticus Finch in *To Kill a Mockingbird* shows bravery on behalf of his client, Tom Robinson. He stands (well, sits) guard outside Tom's cell throughout the night before his trial to protect Tom from any vigilante justice. Does Atticus bring a gun to protect himself? No, only a chair, a floor lamp, and a book, but this lack of firepower does not stop him from standing up to a gun-toting mob that has come to lynch the innocent Black man.

Lawyers are often shown as having become personally involved in their cases and clients. They often go beyond the professional detachment that a lawyer usually maintains and far beyond the attitude that theirs is just another job. Prosecutor Kathryn Murphy in *The Accused* breaks down and cries when rape survivor Sarah Tobias says to her, "I thought you were on my side. You told me you were on my side!" Lawyer Joe Miller, played by Denzel Washington in *Philadelphia*, starts off rejecting the case of the gay AIDS victim because of his fear of AIDS and hatred of homosexuals, but he ends up a virtual member of his client's family. Joe sits on the edge of his client's hospital bed and helps put on his oxygen mask. He buys the Dom Perignon for his client that he would not buy for his wife on the birth of their daughter, he hugs Andrew's partner (played by Antonio Banderas), and he and his wife go to the funeral after his client dies. This is more than most service providers would do for a client. The lawyers in . . . *And Justice for*

All get so involved with their clients that it is hazardous to their health. Jeffrey Tambor plays lawyer Jay Porter. He successfully gets a guilty murderer off on a technicality, after which the freed man kills two kids. Jay tells his friend and colleague that as a lawyer he is "not supposed to feel." But he does feel and slowly goes insane. First he shaves in head, and later he must be dragged from the courthouse, screaming, after commandeering a tray of heavy ceramic plates and pitching them down the hallway at anyone who tries to approach him.

Some lawyers become strongly connected to a case because they identify personally with their client or the victim of a crime. Reggie Love in *The Client* cannot help but feel for her child client because her own children were taken away from her after she was declared an unfit mother on account of her past drinking. Her mother tries to remind her that Mark is just a client, but it is no use. "He's never had a break," the lawyer says, "and he's counting on me." Late in the film, when Mark hugs Reggie tearfully and says he loves her, she replies, "I know, sweet boy, I love you too." Bobby DeLaughter in *Ghosts of Mississippi*, also cannot help associating with the victim of the crime he is prosecuting. He is a father of three, just like the murdered civil rights leader Medgar Evers. When he decides to pursue the case, he is even the same age as Evers was when he died. Bobby asks, "What kind of man shoots another man in the back in front of his family?" He ends up becoming so personally identified with the trial that he strongly resists a special prosecutor being assigned to what he considers his case. Lawyer James Stamphill is the same age as his client Henri Young (Kevin Bacon) in *Murder in the First*, though their lives have gone in totally different directions. In seeing a young man like himself who, because of his unfortunate circumstances, has suffered so much, Stamphill goes from being simply being a lawyer to being a friend. He plays cards with Henri, brings his long-lost sister to visit, and even secures a prostitute, whom he smuggles into Henri's cell as a legal secretary, to assist Henri in losing his virginity. Rudy Baylor in *The Rainmaker* is also around the same age as his client, Donny Ray, who is dying of leukemia. He does more than just prepare a defense for Donny Ray, he takes him out for an afternoon and brings the client home to his kindly landlord and neighbor's home for dinner.

Equally often as they are shown as being hard working, passionate, and committed to their cases and clients, lawyers are also shown to be intelligent, observant, clever, and inquisitive. The lawyer's intelligence is often held up in legal cinema as one of his or her best attributes. Lawyer Fred Gailey in *Miracle on 34th Street* cleverly comes up with a brilliant and completely plausible legal strategy to prove that his client is "the one and only Santa Claus." He gets the district attorney to concede that the U.S. Post Office is an authoritative source and then presents the judges with letters, addressed only to "Santa Claus," that have been delivered to his client Kris Kringle. It allows the court to find that, "Since the United State government declares this man to be Santa Claus, this court will not dispute it. Case dismissed!" Even the morally dubious "Bruiser" Stone, played by Mickey Rourke in *The Rainmaker*, is knowledgeable about the law—he is able to recite from memory the name and citation of the case that will allow for the introduction of stolen evidence at trial. Mitchell McDeere in *The Firm* is clever enough to put together an elaborate plan that will allow him to comply with the FBI's demand that he turn in the members of his firm, retain his ability to practice law by preserving his clients' confidence, hold the mob at bay, and for good measure, even get his brother out of prison.

Many lawyers are shown saving the day, using their keen powers of observation to pick up a detail that everyone else appears to have missed. Kelly McGillis's prosecutor in *The Accused* looks at the high scores on the video game in the bar where the rape of Sarah Tobias took place. She finds a high score that corresponds to the date when the attack happened, and thus finds a missing witness. In *The Client*, after client Mark Sway tells his lawyer that he found mob lawyer "Romey" Clifford after he was dead, his lawyer catches Mark in a lie when he describes Romey as fat and sweaty. "Dead men don't sweat, now do they?" she asks Mark sarcastically. The prosecutor in *The Juror* notices the knowing glance that the acquitted gangster defendant gives to the juror Annie Laird (Demi Moore), prompting the lawyer to approach Annie later and ask her about jury tampering. The title lawyer in *My Cousin Vinny* notices the formation of skid marks on a picture of the parking lot outside the Sac-O-Suds convenience store crime scene, which allows him to determine that they could not have been made by his clients' car. Richard Dreyfuss, as lawyer Aaron Levinsky in *Nuts*, is perceptive enough to notice that in his client's doodles of her family, all the members have no mouths. "Speak no evil," he says, recognizing they are hiding an important secret, namely, the sexual abuse Claudia suffered as a child from her stepfather. Atticus Finch in *To Kill a Mockingbird* notices and points out at trial that the injuries suffered by the assault victim on the right side of her face would have to have been made by a left-handed attacker. His client, Tom Robinson, is right handed, and the woman's father, who appears to have beaten her in the past, is left handed. Ted Danson, as assistant prosecutor Peter Lowenstein in *Body Heat*, begins suspecting that his friend Ned is involved in a murder plot, when he observes that Ned and the victim smoked the same brand of cigarettes. Paul Newman in *The Verdict* ultimately wins the case by reading meaning into a comment made by the nurse who was in the operating room when his client was put in a coma, but who refuses to testify. She tells him, "You guys are all the same. You don't care who you hurt. All you care about is the dollar. You're a bunch of whores!" Putting this comment together with other evidence, he is able to conclude that the loyal nurse is lying to protect the admitting nurse, who was forced by her superiors at the hospital to change records about the patient's aversion to a particular anesthetic. Jim Carrey, as lawyer Fletcher Reede in *Liar Liar*, is forced to win his case by using his smarts (not lies) and notices that his client lied about her age, making the prenuptial contract between her and her husband void. Elle Woods in *Legally Blonde* comes through with not one but two insights that were missed by every other lawyer on the case, including Massachusetts's supposedly best defense lawyer. Elle figures out a witness must be lying when claiming that she was in the shower when a murder took place because she had gotten a permanent earlier that day and, as Elle observes, "The laws of hair care are finite," meaning no water for twenty-four hours after a perm. Plus, Elle can glean from the bitchy comment of another witness ("Don't stomp your little last year's Prada shoes at me, honey!") that he was gay and could not possibly have been having an affair with the defendant as he claimed. "Gay men know designers," Elle observes. "Straight men don't."

More than simply being observant, lawyers are sometimes also shown as being particularly inquisitive. After initially refusing to take the case in *A Civil Action*, lawyer Jan Schlichtmann is nonetheless so compelled to see what is going on at the factories that have been suspected of dumping chemicals that he trudges through the woods in his suit and expensive dress shoes. Vincent Gambini in *My Cousin Vinny* is able to win his case because he is so naturally inquisitive, asking questions throughout the film about such mundane matters as how to cook grits and what it means to get "mud in the tires." This allows him to impeach a witness who misstates the time it took for him to cook his grits and then supposedly see the two defendants enter and leave the scene of the crime. It also allows Vinny to observe tire tracks at the crime scene that are atypical of those cars without "posit traction," which get caught in the mud and have one tire spin and another stand still. While on a business trip in the Grand Cayman Islands in the movie *The Firm*, Mitchell McDeere goes on his own to talk with a diving company about the supposed accident that caused the death of two of the firm's associates. In *JFK*, it is apparently lawyer Jim Garrison's curiosity about the Warren Commission report that leads him to further investigate the president's assassination. Defense attorney Laura Kelly, played by Debra Winger in *Legal Eagles*, describes herself as "curious," using that as the justification of why she attends trials for fun. "Some people go to ballgames, I go to court," she explains.

Some lawyers are shown sprinkling their intelligence with a bit of trickery or even deviousness, but always in service to their innocent client. James Stewart's character in *Anatomy of a Murder*, defense lawyer Paul Biegler, intentionally makes a comment he knows will not be allowed by the judge. He apologizes when it is objected to, and the judge then instructs the jury to disregard the statement. "How can a jury disregard what it's already heard?" Paul's client asks him. "It can't, Lieutenant," he replies. "It can't." (Lawyer Teddy Barnes in *Jagged Edge* uses a similar technique to sneak in the sympathetic testimony of a murder victim's brother.) Biegler is not above carefully placed theatrics or cute tactics, either. He conveniently leaves a homemade fishing lure in a law book that he hands to the judge in chambers, allowing Paul to strike up a chummy conversation about fly fishing and bond with the judge.

He puts a surprise witness on the stand to trap the prosecutor into extracting some helpful information that would have been awkward for Paul to ask about himself. At another point, when the prosecutor objects to a comment of Paul's, saying he ought to know better, Paul apologizes and paints himself as the underdog saying, "I'm just a humble country lawyer trying to do the best I can against the brilliant prosecutor from the big city of Lansing." Tom Logan in *Legal Eagles* resourcefully fakes (OK, lies) his way through an insurance company, posing as an employee to gain access to information he needs from their files. Similarly, Tom Cruise's character in *The Firm* uses a lie to sweet talk his way into the room with the files he needs to prove that the firm is overbilling its clients. James Woods's defense attorney character in *True Believer* does the same thing to get into the manufacturing area of a plumbing supply company to try and find a potential witness. Simultaneously, his newly hired associate "sneaked a peek at the Rolodex" to find the employee's home address, apparently having learned quickly from the master. Julianne Moore as Audrey Woods in *Laws of Attraction* poses as a potential buyer to scope out the townhouse of her client's ex-husband and to search for missing artwork that would factor into the divorce settlement.

Despite the conventional wisdom that lawyers are disreputable, they are also occasionally portrayed in legal cinema as being honest. Lawyer Daniel Rafferty, played by Pierce Brosnan in *Laws of Attraction,* says, "I don't lie. I don't approve of it." In *The Client*, lawyer Reggie Love advises her minor client that he must tell the truth on the stand, even though it may subject him and his family to dangerous reprisal from the mob. "You can't lie," she urges him. "Or you'll be just like them." Jake Weber, as lawyer Curtis Morgan in *The Pelican Brief,* is a whistle blower who loses his life for telling the truth about corporate wrongdoing. Even in *Liar Liar*, a movie that uses lawyers to personify the prevalence of dishonesty in our modern world, there is a portrayal of an honest lawyer. One member of the firm is shown early in the movie telling Miranda, one of the firm's partners, "If you insist that I take [the case] to trial, I will represent Mrs. Cole aggressively and ethically. But Miranda, I won't lie."

Lawyers are often shown as compassionate and tolerant. For every Joe Miller (Denzel Washington) in *Philadelphia*, who early on in the film grits his teeth when he discusses "faggots," admitting, "I'm prejudiced. I don't like homosexuals. . . . I think you have to be a man to understand how really disgusting that whole idea is anyway. . . . I can't stand that shit," there is an Arthur Kirkland (Al Pacino) in . . . *And Justice for All.* Arthur does not so much as flinch when his biologically male, transgendered client, dressed in wig and makeup, puts her hand on his during a pretrial interview. In fact, it is not fair to categorize Denzel's Joe Miller as an intolerant, prejudiced lawyer, either; by the end of the film he completely comes around, having been enlightened by being exposed to the humanity and integrity of a gay man stricken with AIDS. Compassion of a more general sort is displayed by lawyer Aaron Levinsky in *Nuts.* After his client has a particularly wrenching day on the witness stand, confessing to being molested throughout her childhood by her stepfather, Levinsky tenderly comforts her at her bedside, where she lies sedated. "You're supposed to be with the missus," she says to him. "No," he replies, taking her hand, "I'm supposed to be right here." And we see an example of racial compassion and tolerance in the person of Atticus Finch in *To Kill a Mockingbird.* He lives the credo that he preaches to his children, that to understand someone else you "must walk around in another man's skin," and he shows it by voluntarily taking the unpopular case, defending a poor African American man who has been wrongly accused of assaulting a young White woman.

To be fair, there is nothing less than saintly about Atticus Finch—he is surely the most flattering portrayal of a lawyer (and perhaps of a human being) in all of legal cinema. As illustrated previously, he is charitable, tolerant, smart, righteous, and brave. He is a dedicated single father who reads to his children and pines for his deceased wife. He is a competent lawyer, described by another character as being able to "make somebody's will so airtight you can't break it." More important, he is a gentle man who will only play touch (not tackle) football with his son, has never hit his children as long as they can remember, forbids them to fight even when they are being taunted at school because of his case, and will not let his son have a gun. He seems pained even to have to shoot a suffering and dangerous rabid dog. He is downright Ghandi-like in his peacefulness, refusing to fight even when literally spit on by another man. Atticus's goodness is probably the reason he is one of the only fictional lawyers remembered by name by so many movie lovers. Lawyers might be universally hated in America, yet the most memorable and lasting portrayal of a lawyer in legal cinema is this truly noble man.

Some traits commonly associated with lawyers in legal cinema can be either positive or negative, depending on the context. For example, as often as lawyers are shown to be hard working and passionate, they are also shown to be competitive. Whether this love of competition is a good or bad thing depends on how far it drives the lawyer into dishonest or self-serving behavior.

Sometimes a competitive nature is portrayed as a good attribute, pushing lawyers to work hard for their clients and win, which in an adversarial system is vital to proper protection of the innocent. Alan Dershowitz in *Reversal of Fortune* is first seen playing a game of one-on-none basketball and routinely has rough games (keeping track of wins and losses tournament style, of course) with the associates and law students who are holed up in his house to work on the trial. This competitive spirit seems to drive them all. In a conversation with his students, one says, "I agree von Bülow is guilty, but that's the fun, I mean that's the challenge." Dershowitz replies, "See, now there is a lawyer." The lawyer Mitchell McDeere in *The Firm*, shows his competitive spirit in a basketball game as well, yelling, "sonofabitch!" when the opposing team scores a basket. Both the lawyers in *Adam's Rib* appear to be sharpened by their competitive nature. Spencer Tracy's Adam Bonner says to his wife, the confident, aggressive, articulate, fiery, feisty, and equally clever, tough, and driven Amanda, played by Katharine Hepburn with her usual perfect pitch, that he will, "cut you into twelve little pieces and feed you to the jury." In trying to get his innocent client sprung from prison, the defense lawyer in *True Believer* urges his colleague to go beyond simply being satisfied with a battle well fought by reminding him, "A good fight is one you win!" Defense lawyer Teddy Barnes in *Jagged Edge* tells the district attorney, in her desire to get full cooperation during discovery, "If you hold anything back on me, Tom, I'm going to bust your ass wide open." Later she tells him, "I'm going to nail you to the wall." Divorce lawyer Dana Appleton, played by Swoosie Kurtz in *Liar Liar*, tells her opposing counsel

(Jim Carrey), "You want to play hard ball? I'm game!" When divorce lawyer Daniel Rafferty in *Laws of Attraction* tells a reporter that his opponent's case has "about as much chance as a snowball in hell," the opposing counsel, hearing it as a challenge, says to the TV, "OK, Mr. Rafferty, I accept!" Later, the competitive lawyer's mother observes, "You are so adorable when you go in for the kill." Elle Woods's law professor, played by Victor Garber, in *Legally Blonde* encourages his class to compete hard for an internship position at his firm by saying, "Let the bloodbath begin." A love of competition allows for a sort of collegiality between prosecutor Jim Trotter and defense lawyer Vincent Gambini in *My Cousin Vinny*. Trotter says to Brooklynite Vinny, "You did good out there today, Yankee. I like the competition. You like competition, too? Makes things kind of fun, huh?" Vinny replies, "I'm enjoying myself so far." Defense lawyer Paul Biegler in *Anatomy of a Murder* is prodded to take on a case when his friend and colleague Parnell Emmett McCarthy says, "You know something? I think you might be a little bit afraid . . . that you might get licked." After that challenge, of course, Paul cannot help but accept the case.

Competition oftentimes, however, is shown in legal cinema to be a corrupting force in the justice system. District Attorney Frank Bowers, portrayed by Craig T. Nelson in *. . . And Justice for All*, is shown to be arbitrary in his willingness to plea bargain when he tells Arthur Kirkland, "If this was a run of the mill Saturday night killing maybe we could deal. . . . It's the Superbowl and I'm the quarterback!" His ambition and desire to win cloud any motivation to have justice served. "It's a dream come true," he says, "and you're not going to spoil it!" Jessica Lange as the wife of lawyer Sam Bowden, played by Nick Nolte in the new *Cape Fear*, says, "You know how to fight dirty. You do that for a living." The lawyer Leo Drummond, played by Jon Voight in *The Rainmaker*, uses competition to intimidate, as when he offers a settlement to the rookie plaintiff lawyer, played by Matt Damon, and says, "If you say no, it's going to be World War III." Damon's Rudy Baylor expounds on the metaphor later when he compares the sparseness of his travelling accommodations in preparation for a deposition with the luxuriousness of his opponents': "They'll wake up fresh and rested and ready for war."

George Clooney, in a wonderfully over-the-top performance as divorce lawyer Miles Massey in *Intolerable Cruelty*, summarizes his view of litigation and life as, "Struggle, challenge and ultimate destruction of your opponent.... That's life!" On the way to Las Vegas, he tells a stewardess who has predicted he will come back a winner: "I'm going on business. I always win."

Winning, more so than competition, and a blind desire to win above everything else seem to be portrayed in legal cinema as more harmful than the competitive spirit itself. James Stamphill in *Murder in the First* states the hazard of being overly competitive when he says in a voiceover narration, "When you only try to win, you sometimes lose sight of the goal, which should have always been [the client] Henri." Keanu Reeves is Kevin Lomax, who is literally the son of Satan in *The Devil's Advocate*. The devil, in the person of John Milton (get it?), played by Al Pacino suggests to Kevin that he lose a case rather than compromise his morals. Kevin replies and sums up his legal philosophy by yelling, "Lose?! I don't lose! I win! I win! I'm a lawyer! That's my job! That's what I do." Teddy Barnes in *Jagged Edge* tells her potential client, played by Jeff Bridges, "I want to win my case." He asks her whether she won all her cases when she was a prosecutor. "Yes," she replies. "I won every one." She does not say that in one of those cases she was made aware, after the trial, of evidence that would have cleared the man she helped find guilty, leaving open the implication that her desire to keep her winning record may have been a factor in her remaining silent about the truth. Audrey Woods in *Laws of Attraction* admits to "never having lost" a case, and later is reduced to snooping around the office of her opposing counsel. Jennifer Haines in *Guilty as Sin* seems to love competing so much that she does not really care who she represents. After she succeeds in getting a guilty mobster acquitted, she goes to her boyfriend's office and asks him rhetorically, "Is there anything better than winning?" She then proceeds to strip and have sex with him right there and then, illustrating that to her, winning is an aphrodisiac. Later, her boyfriend uses her competitiveness against her when he says, "There's no point talking, Jennifer. You always have to win." Michelle Pfeiffer, as lawyer Rita Harrison in *I Am Sam*, is similarly focused on winning, as evidenced by her statement, "It doesn't matter what I think. It matters that we win." Later on she says, "I've never lost at anything!" The attorneys opposing Paul Newman's Frank Galvin in *The Verdict* stoop to really low tactics, including witness coaching, media manipulation, race politics (in matching Galvin's Black witness with a Black lawyer at their table), and sabotage and spying, having been motivated by the mantra of a senior partner at the firm: "You're not paid to do your best, you're paid to win." Similarly, one of the partners at the firm in *Liar Liar* tells an associate, "Will you let the judge decide what's true? That's what he gets paid for. You get paid to win."

Related to their tendency toward competitiveness, the tendency for lawyers to be ruthless is portrayed as universal to their profession. The title of *The Rainmaker* appears over a shot of sharks swimming in a fish tank, making a clear connection between lawyers and the animal to which they are most often compared. Again, however, ruthlessness can be either a positive or negative trait for the lawyer, depending on degree and context. For the partygoers portrayed in *Regarding Henry*, it is a plus: "Henry represented my cousin three years ago. He was the best, the best! Everyone was terrified." Ruthlessness, for the paralawyer Deck Shifflet, played by Danny DeVito in *The Rainmaker*, appears to make him a more zealous advocate for his client. "There's nothing more thrilling than nailing an insurance company," he says, and it is that sentiment that allows his injured clients to have a lawyer gleefully fighting to get everything they are entitled to—and perhaps more. U.S. District Attorney "Reverend" Roy Foltrigg, played by Tommy Lee Jones in *The Client*, intimidates small-time lawyer Reggie Love, who is defending an eleven-year-old boy, telling her, "You're not equipped to handle this case. You're an amateur, Reggie. You're client is in serious peril—you think that over.... You miss one step, and I'll eat you alive." One viewer might find Reverend Roy to be overly mean, but another might vote for him as someone who is tough on crime. Similarly, the district attorney in *The Juror* can either be seen as wanting to put away evil mobsters at any cost or as going too far when she threatens to leak to the press that compromised juror Annie Laird is bringing charges of jury tampering if she fails to cooperate. Such an action would certainly make Annie and her son vulnerable to reprisal from the gangsters.

Ted Kramer's lawyer, played by Howard Duff, in *Kramer vs. Kramer* goes very hard on the mother of the boy being fought over in this custody case. "I'll have to play rough," he warns Ted up front, and he does not disappoint. When he gets Joanna Kramer (played by Meryl Streep) on the stand, he corners her with the question, "Were you a failure at the one most important personal relationship of your life?" When she won't answer, he yells, "Were you?!" making her literally jump in her seat. Dustin Hoffman as Ted Kramer vocalizes the sentiment of the audience when he later asks his lawyer, "Did you have to be so rough on her?" The lawyer puts it all into perspective by asking back, "Do you want your kid or don't you?" Joanna's lawyer is equally ruthless and sarcastic, saying to Ted, who has discussed on the stand his cut in pay between jobs, "Well, Mr. Kramer, you're the only person I've heard of who is working his way *down* the ladder of success."

Ruthlessness as cruelty appears to be the real sin in legal cinema, and it is portrayed fairly often as a tactic of lawyers. Corporate lawyer Maggie Ward in *Class Action* literally reduces a wheelchair-bound victim in a deposition to tears by showing him pictures of his dead wife and child and blaming him for their death in driving what is actually a dangerously defective automobile, wantonly sold by her client. She similarly humiliates an elderly witness whom she knows is being accurate and truthful and makes him cry on the stand by making him appear easily confused. Frederic March, as lawyer Matthew Harrison Brady in *Inherit the Wind*, is shown betraying the confidence of a witness by questioning her in court about a statement she made to him in a private moment of vulnerability. He badgers her ruthlessly on the stand, stopping only when his wife calls out his name as if to break him from a trance over which he had no control, which has turned him into an unrelenting interrogator. Kevin Lomax in *The Devil's Advocate* has no compunction about tearing apart a molestation victim and making her cry on the witness stand, even though he knows his client is guilty of sexually abusing her. Michelle Pfeiffer in *I Am Sam* reduces the court-appointed psychologist to tears by bringing up her past drug overdose. When one character points out to her, "You made her cry," she responds, "I got lucky." Her opposing counsel, Mr. Turner, played by Richard Schiff, does the same to Sam's kindly neighbor Annie Cassell (played by Dianne Wiest) by bringing up her painful relationship with her father. He also sarcastically belittles Sam's promotion to coffeemaker at Starbucks by saying, "Now after eight years, he can finally make a cup of coffee. Then he can certainly help Lucy with her geography." Janet Venable in *Primal Fear* can be cruel, as when she mimics the speech impediment of Marty Vail's (Richard Gere) client and says, "That st-st-stutter is priceless."

Ruthlessness that is connected to dishonesty, to trying unfairly to get a leg up or to bringing a trial outside of the bounds of fair play, is also portrayed in an unflattering way in legal cinema. This condemnation of lawyers is expressed by Rudy Baylor in *The Rainmaker* when he describes the underhanded tactics used by law students, like stealing library books so other classmates cannot have access to them. "In my first year of law school," he reminisces, "everybody loved everybody else.... By my third year you were lucky if you weren't murdered in your sleep. Such is the nature of the profession." As an illustration, the corporate lawyer in that movie, played by Jon Voight, goes so low as to have the office of his opposing counsel bugged and their phones tapped to gain an upper hand in the courtroom maneuverings. The lawyers of *The Firm* also bug and wiretap the home of their new associate. They also hire a woman to seduce him and then take pictures with which to blackmail him if he should try to divulge the secrets of their illegal money laundering for the mob. If all else fails, there is murder, the fate that befalls four other associates who try to leave after discovering the illegal acts going on there.

The lawyer defending the negligent hospital in *The Verdict*, Edward J. Concannon, played icily by James Mason, is referred to by one character as "the prince of fucking darkness." This ruthless lawyer coaches witnesses and even has a publicity person on staff to get sympathetic articles placed in the local papers and television stations. Most shockingly, he actually hires a woman to seduce, gain the confidence of, distract, and then spy on the plaintiff's attorney. Kevin Lomax in *The Devil's Advocate* illegally eavesdropped on juries from the men's room when he was a young prosecutor, and District Attorney Rufus Buckley, played by Kevin Spacey in *A Time to Kill*, uses political manipulation to get a judge to rule against a motion for change of venue, telling his team of lawyers to "Reach out to our friends in the legislature, have them call on [Judge] Noose. We're gonna help him decide to keep this case in Canton."

The other lawyers at Maggie's law firm in *Class Action* go beyond simple toughness to the point of illegality—a point at which Maggie draws the line. Senior Partner Fred Quinn, played by Donald Moffat (who played morally questionable senior partners in *Regarding Henry* and *Music Box* as well), approves of legally burying evidence in a mountain of files to be sent to the small law firm representing the defendants in what Maggie calls, "Justice by avalanche." He also later okays the illegal destruction of evidence. A more junior member of the firm, played by Jonathan Silverman, asks, "What about the victims?" One of the partners replies, "They should have had a better lawyer." Lawyer Sandy Stern, played by Raul Julia in *Presumed Innocent,* in essence blackmails the judge on a case by threatening to bring up a file that would expose the judge as having taken bribes in the past. The senior partner, Herb Myerson (Tom Aldredge), in *Intolerable Cruelty* tells his junior partner, "We serve the law, we honor the law, and sometimes, counselor, we obey the law. But counselor, this is not one of those times." So they hire a hit man to bump off a client who is about to disgrace the firm. In all these cases, ruthlessness and competition have moved the lawyers beyond toughness and into illegality—something legal cinema does not condone.

Another ambivalent trait often associated with lawyers in legal cinema is the ability to persuade, and even manipulate, with words. In *Hook,* Peter Banning/Peter Pan explains, as he is battling one of the Lost Boys in a competition to see who can come up with the most creative and descriptive insults for each other, "Don't mess with me. I'm a lawyer!" As District Attorney Tom Logan says more directly in *Legal Eagles,* "Carefully chosen words are the tools of my profession." And those tools as portrayed in legal cinema can be used for ill or good. "The silver tongued prince of the courtroom" in *Chicago* is Billy Flynn, played to much-deserved acclaim by Richard Gere. His gift for gab is expressed in a literal tap dance that he is forced to do when an unexpected piece of evidence comes up at trial. In this case, Billy's way with words is probably a plus for his clients but a negative in terms of lawyer portrayals in film, as his words allow him to cloud the truth and take the legal system where he wants it to go, not where the truth would take it. In other cases, however, the eloquence of the lawyer allows for the real truth to come out. The judge in *The Hurricane* admits about the lawyer's argument, "The court is not unmoved by your eloquence and passion," which will eventually lead to a long-overdue acquittal for the unjustly imprisoned man.

In *A Time to Kill*, the day before the closing arguments, in a secret straw poll the members of the jury take among themselves, all of them vote that the client is guilty. It is the passionate and clever summation of Jake Brigance that allows them to get past their racial tunnel vision. He asks the jurors to close their eyes—literally making justice blind—and to imagine the suffering of the little girl who had been beaten and raped by two White thugs. With his carefully chosen words, graphic description, smooth tones, and easy cadence, he paints a mental picture for the jury. Then, for the kicker, he says, "Now imagine that she's Black." In this case, the ability of the lawyer to use words and language to their greatest effect allows for the truth to triumph over prejudice and for all twelve jurors to flip from a guilty to an innocent verdict for the father who took revenge on his daughter's attackers.

The unfeeling or cold demeanor of lawyers could be shown as a necessary attribute to keep a lawyer rational and logical and not unhealthily involved in his or her case. To some degree, we are shown the hazard of losing that objectivity in *Music Box*, where the lawyer played by Jessica Lange agrees to defend her father, who is accused of Nazi war crimes. Her ex-husband advises her not to take the case, saying, "It's not just another case to win." But her brother says, "He ain't no fucking case. He's pop." Her love and emotion end up clouding the facts for a long time, culminating with her statement, "He is not a monster! I am his daughter! I know him better than anyone!" Likewise, in *Jagged Edge*, when Teddy Barnes begins having sex with and then falls in love with her client, she has problems separating the development of the case from her personal feelings. She tells the investigator she is working with (played by Robert Loggia), "Sam, he didn't do it!" Sam replies, "Yeah? Is that your head talking or another part of your anatomy?"

Almost exclusively in legal cinema, however, cold objectivity is shown as a negative attribute—one that keeps the lawyer from helping clients or victims in the way they truly need. Delivering her speech to the graduating class at Harvard Law School in *Legally Blonde*, Elle Woods tells her classmates, "Passion is a key ingredient to the study and practice of law, and life," countering a quote from Aristotle that a professor put on the board during the first day of class: "The law is reason free from passion." Legal cinema seems to take a lawyer's disconnectedness to a case or a client as a negative. Before becoming the admirable lawyer who is emotionally connected to his suffering clients in *A Civil Action*, Jan Schlichtmann is shown as cold and cynical. As a reason for his initial refusal to take the case, he unfeelingly tells the parents who have just told them about the sickness and deaths of their children, "There has to be a defendant, and one with very deep pockets." Rape survivor Sarah Tobias in *The Accused* appears to need and want some support and sensitivity from District Attorney Kathryn Murphy. Instead, she is almost revictimized by the attorney's unfeeling approach to the case. Before expressing even a moment of sympathy or concern for what Sarah has been through, Murphy points out to Sarah that her being drunk and stoned are real obstacles to getting a conviction. She asks, "Were you dressed provocatively?" and "Have you ever made love to more than one man at a time?" She refers to the defendants being released on bail as "standard procedure." Lawyer Rita Harrison in *I Am Sam* is known around her office for being unfeeling. When she tells her colleagues that she has taken a case pro bono, they laugh with disbelief and tease her, "You just spread that love . . . spread it around!" Unfortunately, she is equally cold to her husband and child and has to be taught by her client Sam what it is to love openly and unconditionally.

Sometimes the lawyer's unfeeling nature manifests itself as arrogance or cynicism. At one point in *Music Box*, lawyer Ann Talbot says, "I'm not that cynical." Her ex-father-in-law says, "Yes you are. You're a lawyer, like me." World-weary lawyer Audrey Woods in *Laws of Attraction* is skeptical of every showing of human emotion, saying, "A sincere apology is just a manipulating tactic, like forgiveness or generosity." Defense lawyer Eddie Dodd in *True Believer* dispenses advice to a new hire, telling him, "You want to be a criminal defense attorney? Then know this going in: Everybody is guilty. Everybody!" Billy Flynn in *Chicago* tells it like it is when he says to his client, "You mean only one thing to me... [$5,000]." Another character explains—warns, in fact—"Don't forget, Billy Flynn's number one client is Billy Flynn."

Then there are lawyer traits that are not dependent on situation but are just plain unpleasant, undesirable, antisocial, and nasty, and are portrayed as such in legal cinema. The most prevalent is probably the tendency of the attorney to be arrogant, egotistical, and narcissistic. Billy Flynn in *Chicago* loves his tailored suits and chauffeured Rolls Royce. He proudly declares, "If Jesus Christ had lived in Chicago and if he had $5,000 and if he had come to me, things would have turned out differently." Similarly, in *Primal Fear*, Richard Gere—this time as defense attorney Marty Vail—has no problem telling a client, "I'm what you call a big-shot attorney." He tells a reporter that the only truth that matters is, "My version of it. The one I create in the minds of those twelve men and women sitting on a jury." When the reporter asks him, "When did you know you had them?" he replies, "The day I took the case."

Teddy Barnes in *Jagged Edge* says confidently, "If he didn't do it, I'll get him off." Kevin Lomax in *The Devil's Advocate* brags about being billed out at $400/hr and yells, "I'm too good!" Jan Schlichtmann drives a Porsche, and seems to enjoy driving it very fast, in *A Civil Action*. He is shown getting a speeding ticket in each direction, going to and coming from an interview with his potential clients, as if his ability to pay those tickets puts him above the law and allows him to go whatever speed he wants. Robert Duvall as lawyer Jerry Facher in that same film is equally enamored with his power as a lawyer. "We're like kings," he tells Schlichtmann. "We are kings." Herb Myerson, the senior (very senior—almost decaying, actually) partner in *Intolerable Cruelty*, declares, "This firm deals in power!" His associate, divorce attorney Miles Massey, is openly proud that they spend a whole semester on his prenuptial agreement contract at Harvard Law. "Only love is in mind if the Massey is signed," one lawyer declares. He is also accustomed to being introduced as, "A man whose name is synonymous with bitter disputes and big awards." Although only a law student, Darby Shaw in *The Pelican Brief* is brimming with confidence bordering on arrogance. When a professor asks her why the Supreme Court disagreed with her reading of a case, she replies, "Because they're wrong."

Sometimes the lawyer's arrogance is manifested by paternalism and a disdain for the hoi polloi. Both the lawyers in *Inherit the Wind* are guilty of feeling superior to those involved in the case they are trying. Spencer Tracy as Henry Drummond says, "This community is an insult to the world!" Frederic March as Matthew Harrison Brady tells Henry, "These are simple people, Henry. They work hard and they need to believe in something beautiful." The district attorney, played by John Mahoney, running for reelection in *Primal Fear* says of the people he represents, "Dumb bastards don't even vote. All they want to do is eat, sleep, watch TV and occasionally fuck their wives."

Related to the self-centered nature of the lawyer that is portrayed so often in legal cinema is his or her vanity. The first image of lawyer Miles Massey in *Intolerable Cruelty* is of him at the dentist, getting his teeth whitened. He will examine his teeth in mirrors and polish that beaming smile repeatedly throughout the movie. Matthew Harrison Brady in *Inherit the Wind* seems to love arriving in town as the conquering hero, with him atop a convertible, complete with townsfolk holding signs proclaiming his glory, a band, and the singing of churchwomen to herald his arrival. He glows as he is made an honorary colonel in the state militia, requiring everyone—including the judge—to call him Colonel Drummond for the remainder of the case. Most of all, he loves press attention. One person observes, "Where [Brady] fights, headlines follow." His destruction comes after he is laughed at by members of the community and the media packs up their microphones at the case's conclusion before he can deliver his fiery speech. He bellows to no avail before he collapses and dies, as if dried up from the lack of attention.

Finally, after his momentarily lapse into morality, Kevin Lomax is shown at the end of *The Devil's Advocate* being seduced again into selling his soul by the devil, this time with Satan disguised as a reporter who convinces Kevin to publicly discuss his crisis of conscience. "Vanity," the devil smiles. "Definitely my favorite sin."

The vanity of the lawyer is often evidenced by his or her desire for media attention and fame. "Reverend" Roy Foltrigg in *The Client* is known for his pursuit of media. When it looks like he will be unable to bring a prosecution in a mob case for failure to find the body of the murder victim, the television anchorpeople say, "No front page pictures that Attorney Foltrigg likes so much. No CNN interviews. No speedy ascent to Capitol Hill. Sorry, Reverend Roy." In fact, Foltrigg seems more interested in his press coverage than the case. After an interview in which it appears he has successfully intimidated eleven-year-old Mark Sway into revealing where the body is hidden, he says to his colleagues, "I believe we can do a press conference right here.... You get my makeup off the plane? I'm gonna need pancake No. 7. I think I'll look best behind a bank of microphones." Later on, when Reverend Roy sees himself on TV, he does not mind saying out loud, "I don't look too bad." Lawyer Marty Vail in *Primal Fear* asks a reporter before starting his interview, "This is a cover story, right?" In *True Believer*, defense lawyer Eddie Dodd has his office adorned with newspaper clippings of him fighting for justice, while his opponent, Manhattan District Attorney Robert Reynard (Kurtwood Smith) has his own press clipping in his lobby, crowing about his work busting up drug cartels. When District Attorney Tom Krasny (Peter Coyote) arrives on the murder scene in *Jagged Edge*, the detective meets him outside the house and says, "We got a lot of headlines in there." Jim Carrey, as Fletcher Reede in *Liar Liar*, is asked on the courthouse stairs, "Mr. Reede, do you have a moment?" "I'm sorry," he says. "I'm very late. It's my day to be with my son." That changes, though, when the woman tells him, "A couple of reporters want to talk to you about your big win today." "Oh yeah?" he says, barely pausing. "How's my hair?" When the interview does indeed make him late to pick up his adoring son, he tells the boy, "I ran out of gas!"

Blind ambition and a hunger for power are also widespread traits among lawyers in legal cinema. Warner Huntington III, the boyfriend of Elle Woods in *Legally Blonde*, coldly breaks up with her after years of dating because, "If I'm going to be a senator by the time I'm thirty,... I have to marry a Jackie, not a Marilyn." Everyone seems to know that District Attorney Tom Krasny in *Jagged Edge* has his eye on a senate seat—particularly the defendant, Jack Forrester. When Forrester is accused of murdering his wife, he says, "He's gonna ride my ass into the senate!" When reporters ask him whether they think his being accused of the crime has something to do with Krasny's senate race, Forrester tells the press, "He's an ambitious guy, he has big political aspirations, so I guess you can draw your own conclusions." Another district attorney, Robert Reynard in *True Believer*, goes so far as to frame an innocent man for murder to protect a key informant in a Colombian drug case he was pursuing as a more junior member of the prosecutor's office. He saw the capture of the drug ring, and perhaps the headlines and prominence that resulted, as justification for the imprisonment of an innocent Korean immigrant. "It was a trade-off," he says on the witness stand at the trial seeking to set free the innocent defendant, who has already spent eight years of his twenty-five-to-life sentence. Without remorse, Smith says, "I'd do it again." The head of the sex crimes division in *Presumed Innocent*, Carolyn Polhemus, played by Greta Scacchi, is portrayed as an ambitious Lady Macbeth of sorts. She has an affair with her colleague, Rusty Sabich (Harrison Ford), and urges him to go the district attorney about running for reelection in his place: "He just needs a push." She dumps him when he decides not to pursue that course and then cuts out the middleman by beginning to sleep with the district attorney himself. Jennifer Haines in *Guilty as Sin* started as a paralegal at her firm and clawed her way to the top. Fletcher Reede in *Liar Liar* yells, "How much ass do I have to kiss to make partner in this place?" District Attorney Rufus Buckley, played by Kevin Spacey in *A Time to Kill*, responds to defense lawyer Jake Brigance mistakenly calling him Governor Buckley by saying he is not governor . . . yet. Mitchell McDeere in *The Firm* goes from pizza delivery boy to law student. One character observes, "He must be the most ambitious man in the world." "One of them," his wife replies. This ambition, though, is an attempt to escape the shame he feels for his poor upbringing. "This is about a mother in a trailer park and a [convict] brother you pretend you don't have," his wife insightfully points out to him.

Lawyers are often shown loving wealth as much as power. Kevin Lomax in *The Devil's Advocate* was a prosecutor and got sixty-four straight convictions, but he switched to being a defense lawyer largely for the money. In *The Rainmaker*, when his young client dies from the leukemia that the insurance company would not pay to treat, Danny DeVito as Deck Shifflet arrives at the funeral almost gleefully, saying to his partner, "Now it's a wrongful death suit. Gazillions!"

The money factor is also a contributor to other negative lawyer traits as portrayed in legal cinema. Ambulance chasers are as disdained in movies as they are in real life. *The Verdict* depicts Frank Galvin as totally down and out by showing him paying off a funeral director to make an introduction to a grieving widow so that he might represent her. "He's a very fine attorney," the funeral director says to the woman in black. When he strikes out with her, Frank just goes back to the obituaries in the newspaper to find his next potential client. Lower than an ambulance chaser, even, this guy is a coffin chaser. In *The Rainmaker*, when Rudy Baylor is hired by "Bruiser" Stone, Bruiser says, "You'll see what real lawyers do." In this case that means working exclusively for fees earned on cases won—cases usually found by following up on the accident reports that Bruiser is fed daily by his old friends at the precinct. At first Rudy objects, saying haughtily that at law school, "They didn't teach me how to chase ambulances." His colleague, Deck Shifflet, says matter-of-factly, "Well, you better learn quickly, or you're going to starve." Deck knows everybody at the hospital by their first name, and they know him.

In *The Client*, we also see the ambulance chaser plying his trade—literally. Gill Beale (Will Zahrn) is scurrying around, attempting to scare up clients at the hospital. One patient complains, "More lawyers around this place than doctors." The lawyer almost gets one when Mark Sway needs someone to protect him from the government lawyers who want to question him, but where is the money in that? Gill only does personal injury. The lawyer who comes to defend Tom Hanks's character in *Philadelphia* is also an ambulance chaser of sorts. Joe Miller is known everywhere he goes as "The TV Guy" because of his tacky commercials, in which he tries to solicit clients over the air. In *Wild Things*, Bill Murray plays a deliciously slimy ambulance chaser named Ken Bowden, whose office proudly displays autographed pictures of former clients in neck braces and crutches, smiling and holding checks. Despite his unsavory way of practicing law, however, Ken is not a hack. He is smart and a tough questioner in court. The negativity toward ambulance chasers in film apparently comes from the crass way they attempt to profit from the misfortunes of others, not because they let their clients down. Even these lowlife lawyers are usually portrayed as being quite competent.

There is also no love lost in legal cinema for the lawyer as hired gun, who, like a Nazi prison guard, claims to just be doing his job. In defending a mobster in *Guilty as Sin*, the lawyer played by Rebecca De Mornay says unapologetically, "My job is to get Ed Lombardo off." After she succeeds, he asks her, "What would it take to keep you on retainer?" She bluntly replies, "A lot!" The smooth stalker client played by Don Johnson attempts to get her to take his case by saying, "For every five Lombardos you represent you should take on at least one innocent man." Defense lawyer Eddie Dodd in *True Believer* has his victory diminished when outside the courtroom his coke-dealer client who has just been acquitted says to him, "Amazing horse shit! . . . Eddie Dodd: everyone should own one."

The young, idealistic Rudy Baylor in *The Rainmaker* asks the older, corrupted corporate lawyer, Leo Drummond pointedly in the middle of a deposition, "I'm just wondering, do you even remember when you first sold out?" A lawyer in *The Star Chamber* who gets some seemingly guilty child pornographers off is not redeemed very much when he tells his clients who invite him for a drink to celebrate, "Look, I did my job. The lady who holds those scales is blindfolded. She doesn't have to see who I do it for. However, I do. I checked with the Bar Association and they said I don't have to have a drink with you." Likewise, Mary Steenburgen, as the tough lawyer defending the firm in *Philadelphia*, is not shown as being any more admirable for returning to the defense table after some seedy questioning about the sex life of discrimination victim Andrew Beckett and whispering under her breath, "I hate this case." Marty Vail in *Primal Fear* seems to be grasping at straws when he justifies why he defends scumbag clients. He starts loftily, saying, "Every defendant . . . has the right to the best defense his attorney can provide." But then he gets honest when he says, "I hate when they go on and on about what big fucking whores defense attorneys are. . . . You don't ask, you don't care, you do the goddamn job. It's not like they're your friends, for christsake."

The business aspect of being a lawyer in general is shown as an ugly underbelly of the legal system—a sort of unpleasant reality that people (and audience members) would rather forget than recognize as an integral part to the whole thing. Many movies do not let moviegoers get away with this "don't ask, don't tell" policy. Deck Shifflet bluntly states the facts of life for the legal profession in *The Rainmaker*: "There's a lot of lawyers out there. It's a marketplace. It's a competition." His young associate, Rudy Baylor, knows this reality too well, as he is driving a junky old car and has been evicted from his most recent apartment. Thus, Rudy is considered admirable when he answers the question of his young, dying client, Donny Ray, whether they should take the $75,000 settlement offered by the insurance company. "No way," Rudy advises, knowing he is giving up his fee. "I want to expose these people." This would be considered not noble but stupid if any type of businessman other than a lawyer were to make this decision. Even in *The Rainmaker* it comes to be Rudy's undoing, as he and his partner are forced to close their new firm when their court award bankrupts the defendant and keeps them from getting any real money. *Anatomy of a Murder* makes it clear that lawyer Paul Biegler has been having a problem getting clients—so much so that he can not afford to pay his secretary (the saucy Eve Arden). He balances his need for income with his dislike of a potential client who wants to hire him. His lawyer friend reminds him, "You don't have to love them, just defend them." Similarly, Jake Brigance in *A Time to Kill* is having a hard time paying the utilities on his office because of his lack of clients. He is understandably upset when his client is unable to pay him more than $900 for his defense.

A Civil Action, which is based on a real case, is a kind of cautionary tale of putting principle before solvency. Jan Schlichtmann and his partners lose their firm when they fail to take a settlement and end up being outgunned by the legal resources of two huge corporate defendants. A similar risk is taken by lawyer Ed Masry in going against a utility company in *Erin Brockovich*. One scene shows Erin having to convince some skeptical clients why the firm's 40 percent contingency fee is worth it for them.

Politics is portrayed as an even lower motivator than money in legal cinema, even though it, too, is a very real part of the legal system and a real factor for lawyers to consider. In *Anatomy of a Murder*, Paul Biegler is in the predicament of trying to scramble for clients, perhaps because he did not pay enough attention to politics and lost the election to be district attorney after ten years as the public prosecutor. Politics are very prominent in *Presumed Innocent*, in which the prosecuting attorney, played by Brian Dennehy, is running hard for reelection in the rough-and-tumble world of Chicago politics. He says with resignation, "In the end all you can do is try to hang on to the fucking job." The race increases the pressure on Rusty Sabich to solve his case, with his boss yelling, "If you don't find me a killer there is no fucking office!" It is also Chicago politics in *Primal Fear* that seem to motivate District Attorney John Shaughnessy (John Mahoney) into trying to stifle the sexual abuse angle in a case involving a murdered bishop. "It's [Aaron] Stampler that's on trial, not the Catholic Church," he yells. It was probably politics that moved him to help the archbishop cover up sexual abuse in the past. The question is raised in *Jagged Edge* of whether the district attorney, played by Peter Coyote, is being motivated by a political vendetta when he prosecutes for murder the editor of a newspaper that has been writing very critical editorials about him.

If there is one thing a lawyer is not supposed to be, however, it is dishonest. And if there is one negative trait that Hollywood shows more than any other in lawyers, it is that they lie and encourage others to lie as well. Billy Flynn in *Chicago* completely fabricates a sympathetic background story for his client and a new version of the crime events, and then feeds it to the press. Likewise, Miles Massey in *Intolerable Cruelty* suborns perjury from his client by feeding her his own version of the events surrounding her divorce. He has the gall to characterize it as the truth when he tells her, "The truth is so self-evident to me, Mrs. Donaly, that I am sure that I'll be able to make it equally transparent to any jury." Rita Harrison in *I Am Sam*, attempts to do the same thing with her client, saying to him, "Can you grasp the concept of manipulating the truth? Not lying, just a little tweak here and there?" As previously discussed, James Mason as Edward J. Concannon in *The Verdict* rehearses witnesses to the point of coaching them—unethically leading them to give particular testimony. Michael Grazier (Colin Friels), one of the partners at Maggie's firm in *Class Action*, lies on the witness stand about destroying evidence. Defense lawyer Eddie Dodd in

True Believer goes from saying, "I embellished" to "I embroidered" to finally admitting "I lied," when describing the comments he made to a *Daily News* reporter in an effort to give the appearance of a strong case for his client. At least in this instance it was done in defense of a truly innocent man doing time because he was dishonestly framed for murder. Frankly, though, Eddie appears ready to lie for any of his clients. Early in the film, when he rattles off a case theory to his young associate, the other lawyer asks, "You really think that's what happened?" Eddie replies, "No, but it'll make one hell of an opening statement."

As the title of the film implies, of course, *Liar Liar* is based on the assumption that lawyers lie. Early in the film, we see a young boy explaining to his teacher what his father does for a living. "My Dad, he's a liar.... He wears a suit and goes to court and talks to the judge." The teacher corrects him, "You mean a lawyer!" The child shrugs as if to say, "Same thing." The film goes one better when the lawyer, played by Jim Carrey, explains to his five-year-old son, "Sometimes grownups need to lie.... No one can survive in the adult world if they have to stick to the truth." Of course, this point of view is coming from a habitual, and perhaps pathological, liar, whom it appears will be personally and professionally ruined because he is made incapable of lying for twenty-four hours as a result of his son's magical birthday wish.

Sometimes the lies of lawyers take the form of illegal and unethical activities. District Attorney Tom Krasny in *Jagged Edge* has buried evidence at least twice. The first time, in a case one character dubs, "The kind of case that wins elections, makes careers," he held back information found by one of his investigators that would have exonerated a man who was found guilty of murder. In the case being shown in the film, he has held back a witness statement and pulled a police report, causing the judge to say, "You breached the canon of ethics, Mr. Krasny!... If it was up to me, I'd vote to disbar you!" The managing director of the firm in *The Devil's Advocate*, Eddie Barzoon, played by Jeffrey Jones, routinely shreds documents to protect the firm and his bosses from a government inquiry about the illegal activities in which they are all involved. The managing partner in *The Firm* bribes a clerk in Harvard's placement office to get information on the highest offer to date for the recruit they want the most, and this is probably the tamest wrongdoing going on at the firm. When their new recruit (Tom Cruise) arrives, he tells the lawyer assigned to mentor him (Gene Hackman), "I'm just trying to figure out how far you want [the law] bent." The supervising lawyer answers, "As far as you can without breaking it." "Bruiser" Stone, the lawyer who hires the fresh law school graduate, played by Matt Damon, in *The Rainmaker*, has to leave the country after he is discovered getting involved with jury tampering, running a money-skimming operation, and other illegal activities. Elle Woods's legal intern colleague in *Legally Blonde* suggests Elle tell their law professor and supervisor the information she has, even though she has promised the client she wouldn't. "If you tell him," he suggests," he'll probably hire you as a summer associate.... Think about yourself." "I gave her my word," Elle explains. "Who cares?" the unethical law student replies. The film suggests that the young interns should not be expected to be any better than their professor and supervisor at the law firm, who is not above offering Elle a summer job in exchange for sex. In *A Time to Kill*, Jake Brigance's friend is divorce lawyer Harry Rex Vonner, played by Oliver Platt. Vonner is referred to as "morally compromised," and when he is asked what he would do on a case like Jake's, he replies, "Cheat. Cheat like crazy." That hardly seems out of line in this situation, because the district attorney, played by Kevin Spacey, implies that he may be complicit in some jury tampering when he seems to know the identity of potential jurors before selection even begins, while the defendant's team does not.

Sometimes the illegal behavior of lawyers rises to the level of criminality, even murder. Lawyer Marty Velmano, played by Anthony Heald in *The Pelican Brief*, suggests the "retirement" of two Supreme Court justices to improve the position of his client's case. In this instance, retirement is a euphemism for assassination. William Hurt as sleazy and sloppy lawyer Ned Racine in *Body Heat* agrees to kill the husband of his lover, allowing him to have her and the considerable fortune she stands to inherit. Sean Penn as David Kleinfeld in *Carlito's Way* begins by stealing a million dollars from his mobster client that was meant to pay off a witness. From there, he spirals into money laundering, jury tampering, drug addiction, and murder. He even betrays Carlito, his loyal friend and client, by offering Carlito up to the district attorney as a trade for leniency for himself. "There's only one rule," he rationalizes to Carlito. "You save your own ass!"

Scattered throughout legal cinema, lawyers are shown as possessing other undesirable traits as well. The crooked lawyer Jim Frazier, played by Humphrey Bogart in *Angels with Dirty Faces*, is not only involved with the mob but is a disloyal, two-timing coward. Frazier has his old partner in crime take the rap for a crime they committed together and has him sent to jail under the pretense of building up connections for the two of them, which they can use when his partner gets out in three years. Instead, when the partner is released from jail, the lawyer attempts to have him bumped off. In *Murder in the First*, James Stamphill's (Christian Slater) lawyer brother, played by Brad Dourif, gets leaned on by the Justice Department to help scuttle Stamphill's case. He sets up and sells out his brother James by arranging for a potential witness to be beaten up to intimidate him from testifying.

Other lawyers are also shown to be cowards. The first lawyer shown in *The Client* is Jerome "Romey" Clifford, who is attempting suicide in fear that the mob will get to him because he knows where they have buried the body of an elected official they killed. The district attorney in *The Untouchables* repeatedly tells Eliot Ness (Kevin Costner) that he needs some very strong evidence before he will seek an indictment against Al Capone (Robert De Niro). "I'm not going to go out on a limb!" he keeps saying. "I'm not going to make a fool of myself!" Even the loveable Groucho Marx, as lawyer J. Cheever Loophole in *At the Circus*, is shown to be cowardly, such as when he backs down from questioning the circus strong man for fear of being used as a dumbbell. Ever the gallant rescuer—or at least the woman chaser—however, he regains his courage to help a pretty lady in distress.

Finally, as their least egregious sin, lawyers are occasionally portrayed in film as stuffy and pompous. In *Barefoot in the Park*, Robert Redford, playing a newlywed attorney, is accused by his new wife, played by Jane Fonda, of being "proper and dignified, practically perfect. . . . Before we were married, I thought you slept in a tie." To all this he replies, "That's a rotten thing to say." She finds them incompatible as a couple because he is not enough of a free spirit to be with her. Likewise, the grown-up Peter Pan in *Hook,* lawyer Peter Banning, is a stick-in-the-mud. He yells at his son for playing too loudly, telling him to "stop acting like a child," to which the boy retorts with a smile, "I am a child." When Peter returns to Neverland, the pirate Smee says, "He's forgotten everything," referring not only to Peter's failure to remember his former identity as the boy who wouldn't grow up, but also to his ability to fly, crow, and otherwise act as a rambunctious, carefree child. In the lame courtroom comedy *Trial and Error,* Charles Tuttle, played by Jeff Daniels, describes himself as "very respectable," but like Redford's Paul, his respectability is a straightjacket. He is marrying the daughter of the senior partner, even though he is not in love with her. Like many lawyers, he is a high-strung overachiever who is not very happy with his life and who is destined to become even more unhappy. The turning point comes when he falls for a free spirit and throws his suit into her convertible as he kisses her, symbolizing the throwing away of his old, constrictive respectability.

Overall, however, even with this long list of commonly portrayed shortcomings, lawyering as a profession is shown to be an important element to America's justice system, and even a somewhat noble one. Lawyers may, on the whole, be portrayed in legal cinema as antisocial (workaholic, competitive, tough, etc.), but this is more often than not done in ways that seem desirable or necessary to doing their job effectively as zealous advocates.

Sometimes the negative traits of the lawyer are abandoned by the movie's conclusion, often as part of a redemption that occurs through their practice of the law. The first shot of *The Verdict,* for example, is a silent silhouette of Paul Newman as lawyer Frank Galvin, drinking beer, smoking a cigarette, and playing a pinball machine at a bar. To call him down on his luck would be an understatement. He is an out-of-control alcoholic without any prospects. At one point he staggers through his office and breaks his law degree, symbolizing his inability to do well as a lawyer despite having graduated second in his class from Boston College and having been editor of the law review there. Galvin fell from grace when his partner bribed a juror; he was scapegoated when he threatened to expose the firm. After he left that firm, his wife left him. Now he has a case that can be his salvation. "Maybe I can do something right," he says desperately. He emerges victorious, and at the film's conclusion he is shown drinking coffee instead of alcohol: The practice of the law has been his redemption. Similarly, in *Anatomy of a Murder*, lawyer Parnell Emmett McCarthy (Arthur O'Connell) is portrayed as an alcoholic—perhaps even what used to be known as the town drunk. When his friend Paul Biegler (James Stewart) asks him to assist him on his murder case, Parnell agrees but will only work outside the courtroom. Paul requires him to stay off the booze for the duration of the case. Parnell works hard, even driving north to the Canadian border to investigate and gather evidence. At the film's conclusion, after successfully litigating the case with Paul, he decides to stay sober and return to practice as Paul's law partner. Defense lawyer Eddie Dodd in *True Believer* is shown early in the film frequently smoking pot in his office. He appears burnt out (perhaps in more ways than one) from a decade's worth of defending guilty drug dealers. It is only after weeks of working on a trial to set an innocent client free from prison that Eddie realizes, "You know I haven't gotten stoned once since the trial started." The work involved in attempting to set an innocent man free has apparently given him something more rewarding to focus on. "An innocent man," he muses. "You don't find too many of those in my line of work." Reggie Love in *The Client* is also saved from alcohol abuse through the law, having gotten sober to attend law school and having remained clean for three years. Finally, in *A Time to Kill*, Jake Brigance's mentor is his old law professor, Lucien Wilbanks, played by Donald Sutherland. Wilbanks is now an old drunk—decertified, disgraced, and permanently disbarred for attacking a police officer who busted a picket line. He has vowed never to enter a courtroom again, but in the end he does so to support his former pupil in the case of his life. The practice of law here, even by another, is enough to bring an old legal Lazarus back from the dead.

For some lawyers, the law provides redemption from immoral attitudes and values. In *Class Action*, Maggie Ward sees the true dishonest and ruthless nature of her colleagues and her own amorality while trying a case against her crusading lawyer father (Gene Hackman). She decides to leave corporate law and to work on the side of justice with him. The judge in *Liar Liar* says to lawyer

Fletcher Reede "One more word out of you, Mr. Reede, and I'll hold you in contempt!" After having seen the error of his ways, Fletcher says, "I manipulated the system . . . I hold myself in contempt!" Later he admits, "You know, this truth stuff is pretty cool." In *Philadelphia*, as previously discussed, Denzel Washington's Joe Miller is redeemed, through his practice of the law, from ignorant homophobe to an enlightened, respectable attorney.

When she was with the prosecutor's office, Teddy Barnes in *Jagged Edge* was complicit in information being withheld that would have cleared an innocent man convicted of murder, and it has been eating at her ever since. She had hoped to redeem herself by refusing to do any more criminal law. "Four years ago I walked away from all this," she tells her client suspected of murder. "I felt that I was drowning, over my head. The dirt, the slime! . . . I didn't want to be used anymore. I gave all this up because I just wanted to clean myself." But in fact it is her return to the practice of criminal law for one last case that motivates her to come clean about her unethical behavior years ago. Being exposed again to the seedier side of the law gives the courage to rise above it.

So why are lawyers in legal cinema so often—probably a majority of the time, in fact—portrayed as admirable, capable crusaders fighting for the rights of the downtrodden rather than as the contemptible figures that society normally paints them? Some of it may be just the economics of entertainment: As with the audience proclivity for innocent clients, people do not want to pay for an evening's entertainment focused on a reprehensible charlatan. There may just be too little joy in having negative stereotypes reinforced. Lawyer jokes are fine, but nobody wants to pay to hear them. More likely, though, as was the case with the jury, film is more prone to show the audience's ideal than the reality, or at least its ideal more than its perception.

Legal cinema leaves the lasting impression that even for all their faults lawyers are the defenders of the weak. Chico Marx in *At the Circus* jokes, "Whenever you got business trouble, the best thing to do is get a lawyer. Then you got more trouble but at least you got a lawyer." But when he needs help to save the circus from a scheming scoundrel, he looks in his address book under "T" for "trouble" and finds the name of J. Cheever Loophole, his lawyer.

He knows the lawyer is the defender of the underdog. And why not? Many lawyers in legal cinema expound this exact same philosophy. Ron Silver, as lawyer Alan Dershowitz in *Reversal of Fortune*, says, "If lawyers only defended innocent clients there'd be ten defense lawyers in the entire country.... The system exists for the one innocent person who is falsely accused.... You only got one person who believes in you: your lawyer." Frank Galvin in *The Verdict* says, "The weak have got to have somebody to fight for them." Cher, as lawyer Kathleen Ryan in *Suspect*, says, "I'd do anything for my client. I'm the only chance he has." Lawyer Aaron Levinsky in *Nuts* refuses to be pressured by the judge and opposing counsel into copping a plea for his client. "The accused wants her day in court," he says. "I still believe in that kind of stuff." Eddie Dodd in *True Believer*, says of his clients, "The guiltier he is, the more he needs us." The young Rudy Baylor in *The Rainmaker*, says, "I wanted to be a lawyer ever since I read about the civil rights lawyers in the fifties and sixties.... They gave lawyers a good name." Even the cynical Marty Vail in *Primal Fear*, for all his bluster, secretly confesses, "I believe in the notion that people are innocent until proven guilty.... I choose to believe that not all crimes are committed by bad people. I try to understand that some very, very good people do some very bad things."

In general, lawyers seem to have a deeper respect for the law than any other profession and are shown to be lovers of the law, and perhaps even its guardians. The family of Sam Bowden (Gregory Peck) in the old *Cape Fear* is tempted to take the law into its own hands to combat the evil Max Cady, as expressed by his wife when she says, "A man like that doesn't deserve civil rights." But Sam disagrees: "You can't put a man in jail for what he might do. And thank heaven for that." Similarly, James Stewart, as attorney Ransom Stoddard in *The Man Who Shot Liberty Valence*, will not buy a gun, much less use one to stop the vicious gunslinger Liberty Valence, who wants him dead. "You can't shoot back with a law book," the publisher and editor of the local newspaper warns, but Ransom sticks to his guns—or, more accurately, sticks exclusively to his law. Later he is praised as, "A man who came to us not packing a gun but carrying instead a bag of law books." Paul Biegler (again James Stewart) and his lawyer friend, Parnell Emmett McCarthy, in *Anatomy of a Murder* love the law so much they read judicial opinions every evening for fun. Parnell espouses his "love for the smell of the old brown books." When he approaches them in Paul's law library, he muses lovingly and poetically, "Here's the rose, the lily! Sweet lumen. The United States Supreme Court Reports." Christine Lahti is a lawyer in . . . *And Justice for All* who professes, "I was in love with the law." Even the tempered idealist Rudy Baylor in *The Rainmaker*, who has seen the law at its worst, admits, "I still love the law. I'll always love it." Attics Finch gives his credo to the jury when he says, "In this country, our courts are the great levelers. In our courts, all men are created equal. I am no idealist to believe firmly in the integrity of our courts and our jury system. That is no ideal to me—that is a living, working reality!" And Tom Hanks's Andrew Beckett, in *Philadelphia*, says, "I love the law. I know the law. . . . What I love most about the law? Every now and again . . . you get to be part of justice being done. That really is quite a thrill when that happens."

The lawyers of legal cinema, above all else, believe that the law is the best system of achieving justice in our society. The audience wants to believe this as well. Is it any surprise that the two meet on the silver screen? Who is legal cinema to dash the hope of every American that our court system is the key to a fairer, freer society and nation? Not even a mountain of cynical lawyer jokes can crush that ideal.

Conclusion: Summary Judgment

If legal cinema shows us anything, it is that the law is everywhere. As John Milton (Al Pacino) explains in *The Devil's Advocate*, "The law puts us into everything. It's the ultimate backstage pass. It's the new priesthood, baby. Did you know there are more students in law school than there are lawyers walking the earth? We're coming out! Guns blazing!" Should we be surprised, then, that the law has made its mark up and down the history of cinema? Although the prevalence of law films has seemed to increase as the number of lawyers in America and our nation's litigious tendencies have increased, the earliest film discussed in this book was released in 1938, just a decade after the birth of the talkie. There are at least two movies from each decade after that first film that are also discussed here. Legal films are so pervasive that they have become self referential. In one shot in *Jury Duty*, Pauly Shore does a none-too-shabby imitation of Al Pacino from *...And Justice for All* when he stands up in the jury box and yells, "You're out of order! No, you're out of order!" As discussed earlier, the entire film is a comic twist (albeit an only marginally successful one) on *Twelve Angry Men* and has the lead character pilfering lines from that movie to demonstrate to another character his passionate belief in the innocence of the accused. Sean Penn as Sam Dawson in *I Am Sam* gives an impassioned speech from the witness stand arguing for why he would be a good parent to his daughter if allowed to retain custody. It sounds convincing if perhaps a little familiar. We find out why when one of his friends stands up in the gallery to inform us that it is Dustin Hoffman's speech from the witness stand in *Kramer vs. Kramer*. Apparently, legal cinema has made such an imprint on our collective consciousness (including on this mentally challenged client) that it can provide a cultural shorthand.

One reason for the ubiquity of the law throughout cinematic history has to be the inherently theatrical nature of the trial. By virtue of its structure, it has an introduction in the lawyers' opening statement, a plot and dramatic build-up throughout the presentation of evidence and testimony, and a denouement or finale in the form of the verdict. Sentencing can sometimes be considered the epilogue. There are even intermissions of a sort when the trial recesses or shifts from the plaintiff's/prosecutor's case presentation to the defendant's. There is a director (the judge), players (the lawyers and witnesses), and a built-in, captive audience (the jury). One might argue that the lawyers' job is to paint their client as the protagonist or antagonist in the unfolding drama. Director Taylor Hackford (*The Devil's Advocate*) observed as much in his DVD commentary from that movie: "The courtroom has become the gladiator arena of the late twentieth century. Following the progress of a sensational trial is a spectator sport. You're watching something that's part melodrama, part vaudeville and part cold-blooded calculation." The lawyer character in *...And Justice for All* played by Al Pacino declares, "It's a show! It's *Lets Make a Deal*!" It makes perfect sense that this forum, so artificial and so naturalistic at the same time, should be used so often by filmmakers who want to create make-believe drama in a realistic setting.

There is also a bevy of philosophical angst to explore in turning an audience's attention to the legal system, always a tempting treasure trove to an artist. Existential questions of truth, morality, identity, class, survival, and obviously, justice are ripe to be explored. The imperfection of our legal system in itself is enough to provide sufficient fodder for a body of films. "Paralawyer" Deck Shifflet, played by Danny DeVito in *The Rainmaker*, puts it succinctly: "It's got all twisted, didn't it? This legal profession." As lawyer Henry Drummond, played by Spencer Tracy, in *Inherit the Wind* says, "I've been a lawyer long enough to know here are no total victories anywhere.... [It's] not as simple as all that, good or bad, black or white, day or night." Imperfection leads to introspection, and introspection leads to art.

Truth and honesty weigh heavily as concepts to be grappled with throughout legal cinema. When the grandfather who raised lawyer Arthur Kirkland (Al Pacino) in ... *And Justice for All* asks him, "Are you a good lawyer? Are you honest?" Arthur must reply, "Being honest doesn't have much to do with being a lawyer." Later he tells a jury, "What is justice? ... The intention of justice is to see that the guilty people are proven guilty and the innocent are set free.... Justice is ... the finding of the truth." As the prosecutor in *My Cousin Vinny* (Lane Smith) reminds the jury and the audience, "Truth, that's what verdict means." However, Robert Duvall as lawyer Jerry Facher in *A Civil Action* tells an attorney colleague, "You've been around long enough to know that the courtroom isn't the place to look for the truth." The lawyer in *Primal Fear* refers to it as, "The illusion of truth." Former lawyer Parnell Emmett McCarthy (Arthur O'Connell) tells his friend and colleague Paul Biegler, in *Anatomy of a Murder*, "Maybe you're too pure, Paul, too pure for the natural impurities of the law." The prosecutor in *Trail and Error* accuses her opposing counsel of viewing as indistinguishable the dishonest defense he has put up on behalf of his client and the truth: "You don't care," she says. "It's all the same, right? Truth, lies, lies, truth." The place that truth should have in our legal system is a recurring theme in legal cinema that to some degree justifies the genre's existence all on its own.

Legal cinema seems most of the time to reflect a societal ambivalence about our own adversarial system of justice. America's legal system requires lawyers to win at almost any cost, or at least to fight as hard as they can and then leave fairness up to the judge and truth up to the jury. The theory is that the truth will be best and most thoroughly rooted out if each side has a person fighting with no interest other than doing everything he or she can to get the client what the client wants. Appropriately for the United States, it is a model very much based in a belief in capitalism: Competition is the motivation for hard work that will lead to the most effective and pure outcome. Unfortunately, America seems to have created this inherently combative system and yet expects lawyers to be noble and interested in the finding of the truth, even if the finding of that truth is harmful to the client. This is an inherently contradictory expectation, and legal cinema reflects how difficult it is for society to have it both ways. For example, the judge in *Jagged Edge* reminds lawyer Teddy Barnes (Glenn Close) that, "[The lawyer] took an oath. He must live up to that oath." Barnes then asks, "What if he finds that he can't?" Without apology, the judge says, "Then he has no business taking the oath in the first place." Later, Teddy's client asks her, "How can defend me if you think I'm guilty?" She deadpans, "It happens all the time. It's the way our legal system works."

The movie ...*And Justice for All* squarely laid out the problem back in the 1970s. In the film, Arthur Kirkland explains to the jury, "Both sides want to win ... regardless of the truth and regardless of justice, regardless or who is guilty or innocent. Winning is everything!" What conclusion can he come to except his famous line to the judge: "You're out of order! You're out of order! The whole trial is out of order!"

The end result of that adversarial system is shown visually in *Primal Fear*. The client of attorney Marty Vail has totally manipulated the legal system as well as his lawyer. Marty, who is used to being the puppet master, pulling the strings of justice on behalf of his clients, has been made the dummy in this case. He was cynical about the legal system to begin with, saying to a reporter early in the film, "If you want justice, go to a whorehouse. If you want to get fucked, go to court." But this is mainly a façade—an armor this lawyer puts on to do his job of sometimes defending guilty people. Even he is shocked and conflicted, however, at how justice in his case has been so twisted. One of the final shots of the movie comes from an overhead camera looking down at Marty as he leaves the empty courtroom into the comparatively bright, gray light of a cloudy day. As he walks under the camera and out the courthouse doors, the camera follows him, putting an upside-down picture of the courtroom on the screen. Justice has literally been turned on its head. The last shot is of Marty stopping dead in his tracks outside the court, looking dazed, rumpled, and lost. What is he to do now with truth and justice? Cut to black.

Some films go so far as to lay out an alternative approach, one where lawyers are free to be true to truth, justice, and their conscience—not at all the American way, as least as our legal system goes. *The*

Devil's Advocate literally equates the lawyer's job of knowingly defending guilty clients with selling one's soul to the devil: The lawyer's fee is called "blood money" in this film. Director Taylor Hackford explains in his DVD commentary: "Now that audiences have seen televised trials, they realize that morality and justice has very little to do with the outcomes. The winners are the lawyers who stop at nothing. I thought it would be interesting to put that behavior into a larger context of right and wrong." The Martin Scorsese version of *Cape Fear* is very modern in the plot twist it adds to the original story. In this updated version of the film, lawyer Sam Bowden is not just a bystander who happened upon the evil Max Cady attempting to rape a woman in a parking lot one night but is Max's old lawyer, who defended Cady on rape charges. When he was a public defender, Sam listened to his conscience and buried a report showing that the rape victim was promiscuous, which would likely have let Cady go free. Sam soon after his experience with Cady left the public defender's office because he felt he could not serve his clients and the law at the same time. Even so, Max is right to have expected his lawyer to have done everything to fight for him even if he was guilty. At gunpoint in a mock trial, Max finds Sam guilty of serving not only as lawyer, but also as judge and jury in reaching a conclusion about his client's guilt and acting on it. Did Sam do the right thing? As a lawyer in America's adversarial system, clearly not. But as a person, as a human being? America remains conflicted about that conclusion.

America also remains uneasy about how money plays into our legal system, a misgiving reflected in legal cinema. First, there is lingering discomfort, particularly in our sue-happy modern age, about the fact that the way one achieves justice is through money. As Robert Duvall puts it in *A Civil Action*, "The idea of criminal court is crime and punishment. The idea of civil court and of personal injury law by nature... is money." That film begins with a cold recitation by lawyer Jan Schlichtmann about how much injured clients are worth in our civil justice system, with children being the least. He describes the "perfect victim" as a middle-aged man, "at the height of his earning potential, struck down in his prime." However, this type of valuation seems to be an open secret about which Americans seem to feel guilty, like a shameful skeleton in our collective family closet. The grieving mother in *The Rainmaker* is asked by the lawyer defending the insurance company that deprived her son of the coverage he needed to stay alive what she will do if she receives the multimillion dollar award she is seeking, implying that she is greedy for even asking for it. The jury and audience would probably both tend to agree if she gave the answer that would comport with the true nature of our civil justice system: "I want the money to hurt you and make me feel better about losing my son because of your company's wrongdoing." Instead, to preserve her nobility, the filmmakers have her answer that she will donate it all to a charity that deals with leukemia: "I don't want a dime of your stinking money," she says.

America also remains concerned with verdicts being bought and sold to the highest bidder, or justice only going to those who can afford it by paying for a talented lawyer. This conflict was even symbolized in the Old West in *The Life and Times of Judge Roy Bean.* When Roy proclaims himself a judge, he says, "That brothel there, that'll be my courthouse, the place to deal out justice." Later he shows how he will pimp out justice when he says to some outlaws whom he later deputizes as marshals, "Ordinarily I'd take you in my courtroom and try ya and hang ya. But if you got the money for whiskey, we can dispense with those proceedings." Jack Warden as law professor Mickey Morrissey in *The Verdict* explains that, "The court doesn't exist to give [clients] justice. The court exists to give them the chance to justice."

The legal system is also questioned occasionally in legal cinema as an arbitrary set of rules that stand in the way of real justice being done. An exchange in *The Life and Times of Judge Roy Bean* illustrates the conundrum. "The law is on his side," says one character. "The law!" the other retorts in disgust. "Yes, the law. I didn't say nothing about justice." In *The Hurricane*, there is ample evidence to prove that Rubin Carter has been wrongfully imprisoned. Still, because the state court system is still comprised of the same crooked players who framed him in the first place, and the federal court system is not supposed to hear a case decided in state court, Carter appears to be without legal recourse. He must beg the court, "Do not ignore the law. Embrace that higher principle for which the law was meant to serve. Justice, that's all I ask." Although Rubin finally achieves the justice he seeks, the fact that he is bucking the odds to get around the inflexible and seemingly arbitrary rules of civil procedure makes the audience question the efficacy of a system in which technicalities let an injustice persist for so long.

Still with all the perceived imperfections in the American legal system, it is somewhat counterintuitive that legal cinema would leave the lasting impression that our system is one that produces justice, especially for the weak who have been wronged. As has been explored throughout this book, far more often than not the clients are the innocent victims or underdogs in need of a legal system to protect them from injustice. The judge, by and large, is portrayed as the neutral umpire who keeps the whole process fair. Juries are the invisible arbitrators who make their decisions in silence and mystery, without any appearance of biases or agendas of their own other than seeing justice served. Even lawyers, so disdained in American society, are far more often shown as intelligent, passionate, tenacious fighters for justice for their clients than they are as dishonest, money-grubbing guns for hire.

There are, of course, plenty of exceptions. The days of Tammany Hall and Prohibition-era gangsters allowed for the unflattering portrayal of crooked judges and lawyers in *Angels with Dirty Faces.* The age of twisted justice under Joseph McCarthy produced *Anatomy of a Murder,* the story of a man who gets away with murder as temporary insanity; *Inherit the Wind,* where one lawyer declares, "Fanaticism and ignorance is forever busy and needs feeding!"; and even to some degree *To Kill a Mockingbird,* in which prejudice and ignorance lead to a miscarriage of justice. The counterculture skepticism of the late sixties and early seventies, fed by the Watergate scandal, produced *...And Justice for All,* a scathing black comedy about the failures of our legal system, with its theme song being "Something Funny's Going On." The greed of the go-go Reagan years of the eighties led to *Jagged Edge,* in which a rich and powerful client gets away with the murder of his wife, and *New Jack City,* in which a powerful drug lord gets to cop a plea to a ridiculously low sentence for his many crimes. "Don't get mad," says the arrogant Nino Brown. "It's the law. Sucks, huh?" The O. J. Simpson trial raised concerns about racial prejudice in the legal system on one hand and the ability to buy justice and manipulate the system through theatrics on the other, and in subsequent years it created films like *Chicago*, where one defendant who will get away with killing her lover sings, "Who says murder is not an art?"; *A Civil Action*, where the better financed defendants will use their resources to simply overpower the smaller firm representing the real victims; *The Devil's Advocate*, run amok with evil lawyers who seemed thrilled to be representing gulity clients who can afford their legal fees; *Primal Fear*, where a clever, charismatic defendant who is a good actor fools the jury and the entire legal system; *Wild Things*, another tale of the guilty going free; and tales like *The Juror* and *Runaway Jury* of corrupted juries who have agendas other than finding the truth.

Alongside all these films, however, we have justice triumphing thanks to the legal system in *The Accused, Class Action, The Client, Erin Brockovich, Ghosts of Mississippi, The Hurricane, I Am Sam, Murder in the First, Nell, Nuts, Philadelphia, The Rainmaker, Suspect, A Time to Kill, True Believer, Twelve Angry Men, The Untouchables, The Verdict*, and even *Miracle on 34th Street, My Cousin Vinny*, and *Legally Blonde*. Even in the films mentioned above that have less-than-glowing portrayals of the legal system and the players within it, there are almost always balancing characters and situations showing hope and faith in our legal system. For example, even with a verdict that is clearly a miscarriage of justice, *To Kill a Mockingbird* is remembered as a film about a good lawyer, not about a wronged client.

Apparently our desire to have the legal system that we want and that we have idealized as a society portrayed on the screen, and the pleasure we take in seeing it presented as such, has helped spur an entire genre of legal cinema, for that is what we see when we look at legal cinema as a whole. Clearly deliberations will continue for years to come, likely for as long as there is commercial cinema, including the chicken-and-the-egg question of whether film changes society's perception of its legal system or whether it reflects that view. It seems clear, however, that, beyond either of those tendencies, legal cinema first and foremost is the cinematic representation of our American dream of fairness and justice manifested through the civilized order of our legal cinema. On that question, the verdict is in and it is in favor of hope. Court is dismissed. Roll credits.

Appendix: Order in the Court

Below is a list of the legal films mentioned throughout this book. Listed with each film is the year of its release, the director, the screenwriter(s), and a plot summary, including the names of the actors portraying the prominent legal characters.

The Accused (1988)
Directed by Jonathan Kaplan
Screenplay by Tom Topor

Prosecutor Kathryn Murphy (Kelly McGillis) goes after not only the men who gang raped Sarah Tobias (Jodie Foster) in the back of a rough-and-tumble bar, but also the spectators who stood by and cheered on her attackers. Foster's performance, for which she received her first Academy Award, is the standout element in this otherwise one-note film that has power and relevance primarily because of its subject matter.

Adam's Rib (1949)
Directed by George Cukor
Screenplay by Ruth Gordon and Garson Kanin

Married lawyers Amanda (Katharine Hepburn) and Adam (Spencer Tracy) Bonner enter into a legal battle of the sexes on opposite sides of a criminal trial, where a hapless housewife, played by Judy Holliday, is accused of trying to murder her abusive, philandering husband. Hepburn and Tracy are charming, but the dated comedy delivers few laughs today.

Anatomy of a Murder (1959)
Directed by Otto Preminger
Screenplay by Wendell Mayes

James Stewart as lawyer Paul Biegler teams up with his friend, Parnell Emmett McCarthy (Arthur O'Connell), a former lawyer, to defend a soldier (Ben Gazzara) accused of killing the man who raped his wife. The prosecutor is played by George C. Scott in one of his earliest film roles. A legal film noir that must have been somewhat scandalous in its day, still captivates with its sharp dialogue, excellent performances, and deliberate pace. Fine touches, like credits by Saul Bass, a jazz soundtrack by Duke Ellington, the casting of real-life lawyer Joseph Welch as Judge Weaver, and Preminger's excellent choice to film in black-and-white, add to the film's depth.

...And Justice for All (1979)
Directed by Norman Jewison
Screenplay by Valerie Curtin and Barry Levinson

Lawyers played by actors including Al Pacino, Jeffrey Tambor, Craig T. Nelson, and Christine Lahti try to navigate the chaos of a seventies big-city courthouse, while trying cases in front of crooked and crazy judges like those played by John Forsythe and Jack Warden. A very dated, but still humorous, black comedy with sledgehammer social commentary. The film's verdict on the legal system of its time? In the now famous words of Pacino's Arthur Kirkland, "The whole trial is out of order!"

Angels with Dirty Faces (1938)
Directed by Michael Curtiz
Screenplay by John Wexley and Warren Duff

The saintly Father Connelly (Pat O'Brien) tries to keep the neighborhood street toughs, played wonderfully by the Dead End Kids, on the straight and narrow, while they worship Connelly's childhood friend, gangster Rocky Sullivan (James Cagney). Rocky's partner is the two-timing lawyer Jim Frazier (Humphrey Bogart).

A mostly forgotten classic that manages to both create pathos and inspire hope with its tale of redemption. Uniformly great performances, with Cagney's being particularly memorable.

At the Circus (1939)
Directed by Edward Buzzell
Screenplay by Irving Brecher

A circus worker (Chico Marx) calls his lawyer, J. Cheever Loophole (Groucho Marx), to help save the circus from unscrupulous gangsters. One of the Marx Brothers' less inspired films.

Barefoot in the Park (1967)
Directed by Gene Saks
Screenplay by Neil Simon

A young lawyer (Robert Redford) marries a free spirit played by Jane Fonda who attempts to liberate him from his buttoned-down ways. An adaptation of the Neil Simon play that, though amusing, unfortunately comes off a bit too much like a play on film.

Batman Forever (1995)
Directed by Joel Schumacher
Screenplay by Lee Batchler & Janet Scott Batchler, and Akiva Goldsman

The caped crusader (Val Kilmer) and Robin (Chris O'Donnell) take on The Riddler (Jim Carrey) and former district-attorney-turned-psychopath Harvey "Two-Face" Dent (Tommy Lee Jones). This episode in the Batman franchise of films is more comedy than adventure, and works to a degree on that level.

Body Heat (1981)
Directed by Lawrence Kasdan
Screenplay by Lawrence Kasdan

Sleazy, incompetent lawyer Ned Racine, played by William Hurt, murders the husband of his lover (Kathleen Turner) so that they can continue their torrid affair unfettered and in the splendor provided by the substantial fortune she stands to inherit. Racine's prosecutor friend, Peter Lowenstein (Ted Danson), begins to suspect his friend is involved in something nefarious. A legal technicality provides an important plot point. Sultry but somehow dated, the film is more mood than substance.

Cape Fear (1962)
Directed by J. Lee Thompson
Screenplay by James R. Webb

Lawyer Sam Bowden (Gregory Peck) tries to protect his family from Max Cady (Robert Mitchum), a sadistic rapist recently released from prison, who is stalking Bowden's family as revenge for Sam's role in helping to put Cady behind bars. A somewhat tedious but nonetheless skillfully made film noir classic, with Mitchum creating one of the screen's all-time evil villains.

Cape Fear (1991)
Directed by Martin Scorsese
Screenplay by Wesley Strick

An over-the-top remake of the 1961 thriller. Important for legal film scholars, however, because Sam Bowden (Nick Nolte) is not simply a lawyer who coincidentally acts as a witness to put a bad man in jail, but is lawyer to Robert De Niro's Max Cady, and out of a crisis of conscience intentionally withheld evidence that might have gotten his client off. The plot is an interesting take on the moral difficulties involved in the lawyer's oath to defend his client to the best of his abilities, but is mostly overshadowed by the implausibility of Cady's superhuman abilities, the overwrought family dynamics in the Bowden household, and Scorsese's stylistic directing, which, though usually pitch perfect, this time goes way too far.

Carlito's Way (1993)
Directed by Brian De Palma
Screenplay by David Koepp

Carlito Brigante (Al Pacino) begins the movie as a client in court, being sprung from prison on a technicality after serving five years of his thirty-year sentence. He works hard to stay on the straight and narrow, but past history and his loyalty to his despicable attorney, David Kleinfeld (Sean Penn), seem determined to suck him back into a life of crime. A sort of modern Greek tragedy disguised as a gangster film, and a captivating drama about fighting fate and circumstance. Great performances, and eminently watchable.

Chicago (2002)
Directed by Rob Marshall
Screenplay by Bill Condon

In 1920s Chicago, playboy lawyer Billy Flynn (Richard Gere) defends sexy celebrity murderesses Velma Kelly (Catherine Zeta-Jones) and Roxie Hart (Renée Zellweger) in this splashy legal musical, the big screen version of the Broadway hit by composer John Kander and lyricist Fred Ebb. A very deserving winner of the Academy Award for best picture, all the more significant because it is the first musical since *Oliver* in 1968 to achieve such an honor. Stand-out performances all around, with an Oscar nomination for Zellweger and a well-deserved Oscar win for Zeta-Jones.

A Civil Action (1998)
Directed by Steven Zaillian
Screenplay by Steven Zaillian

The true story of attorney Jan Schlichtmann (John Travolta) and his small firm taking on corporate giants who poisoned the water supply of the town of Woburn, Massachusetts. Robert Duvall plays Jerome Facher, a veteran corporate lawyer, and John Lithgow plays Walter J. Skinner, a morally ambiguous judge. A well-crafted but ultimately unsatisfying film with an unusual amount of legal detail, particularly involving the instruction to the jury.

Class Action (1991)
Directed by Michael Apted
Screenplay by Carolyn Shelby & Christopher Ames, and Samantha Shad

Crusading lawyer Jedediah Tucker Ward (Gene Hackman) takes on his daughter, legal gun-for-hire Maggie Ward (Mary Elizabeth Mastrantonio), in a case against an auto manufacturer accused of knowingly making fatally defective cars. Matt Clark plays the judge, Donald Moffat plays another of his great roles as a corrupt senior law partner, and Larry Fishburne plays one of Hackman's associates. Hackneyed and no-frills, perhaps, but the film still somehow manages to be completely enjoyable, probably because of the family dynamics played so well between Hackman and Mastranonio.

The Client (1994)
Directed by Joel Schumacher
Screenplay by Akiva Goldsman and Robert Getchell

Rookie solo practitioner Reggie Love (Susan Sarandon) gets in over her head defending her young client Mark Sway (Brad Renfro) who knows where the mob has buried the body of a slain U.S. Senator. Tommy Lee Jones plays the colorful "Reverend" Roy Fultrain, the ambitious U.S. Attorney who can be controlled only by the folksy Judge Harry Roosevelt (Ossie Davis). Other lawyers on Fultrain's team include Bradley Whitford. A taut and tender legal thriller, and one of the best films made from a John Grisham novel, in no small part thanks to the terrific performances by Sarandon, Jones, and young Brad Renfro.

The Devil's Advocate (1997)
Directed by Taylor Hackford
Screenplay by Jonathan Lemkin and Tony Gilroy

The devil in the person of lawyer John Milton (Al Pacino) brings the conceited young hotshot Kevin Lomax (Keanu Reeves) into his powerful and corrupt law firm. One of Milton's associates is played by Jeffrey Jones in a wonderfully sleazy performance. Thankfully, Al Pacino is given free rein to chew up the scenery. A legal horror film (perhaps the first) that is stylistic, even over-the-top, in a self-aware kind of way, and very enjoyable as a result.

Erin Brockovich (2000)
Directed by Steven Soderbergh
Screenplay by Susannah Grant

The real-life story of paralegal Erin Brockovich (Julia Roberts) who, with her lawyer boss Ed Masry (Albert Finney), takes on corporate giant PE&G in a class action suit where the utility company is accused of tainting the water supply of the town Hinckley, California. A thoroughly satisfying David-and-Goliath legal tale, with appropriately understated directing by Soderburgh and fine performances by both Roberts and Finney. Roberts, in fact, won an

Oscar for her role. The judge in the real case, Judge LeRoy A. Simmons, plays himself in the film.

The Firm (1993)
Directed by Sydney Pollack
Screenplay by David Rabe, and Robert Towne & David Rayfiel

Ambitious young lawyer Mitch McDeere (Tom Cruise) is recruited for a cult-like, boutique law firm in New Orleans. The closeness of the firm covers dark secrets involving its work on behalf of some highly disreputable clients. Hal Holbrook plays senior partner Oliver Lambert, Gene Hackman is the conflicted lawyer assigned to mentor young Mitch, and Wilfred Brimley plays the ominous head of security at the firm. A clever and exciting thriller adapted from another John Grisham novel.

Ghosts of Mississippi (1996)
Directed by Rob Reiner
Screenplay by Lewis Colick

The true story of a white supremist (James Woods) finally brought to justice for the murder of civil rights leader Medgar Evers (James Pickens Jr.). Whoopi Goldberg plays Evers's widow, who never gives up her fight to achieve justice for her husband's assassination. The film staggers quite a bit under its own self-righteous weight, but the performances of Alec Baldwin as lawyer Bobby DeLaughter and Woods are good, especially Woods, who was nominated for an Oscar.

Guilty as Sin (1993)
Directed by Sidney Lumet
Screenplay by Larry Cohen

Don Johnson plays a suave but psychopathic client who stalks and terrorizes his successful, ambitious, workaholic attorney (Rebecca De Mornay). Dana Ivey has a small role as a judge. A preposterous film, though Johnson does his best to keep it afloat with an oily charm.

Hook (1991)
Directed by Steven Spielberg
Screenplay by Jim V. Hart and Malia Scotch Marmo

Corporate lawyer Peter Banning (Robin Williams) must return to Neverland, rediscover his former identity as Peter Pan, and tap into his inner child to rescue his children from Captain James S. Hook (Dustin Hoffman). The film starts with a cute and clever premise, but it panders to kids and gets too sticky sweet to provide much real magic.

The Hurricane (1999)
Directed by Norman Jewison
Screenplay by Armyan Bernstein and Dan Gordon

The true story of Rubin "Hurricane" Carter (Denzel Washington), a boxing champion framed by a racist police detective for three murders he did not commit, and the young man and his adult guardians who work to free him from prison after having served twenty years. Rod Steiger does a typically quirky turn as a judge. The film would be no less captivating if it were completely fictional, but it is all the more engrossing because it is true. Washington's Oscar worthy performance garnered only a nomination.

I Am Sam (2001)
Directed by Jessie Nelson
Screenplay by Kristine Johnson and Jessie Nelson

An intense lawyer, Rita Harrison (Michelle Pfeiffer), learns to prioritize the important things in her life through her defense of Sam Dawson (Sean Penn), a mentally retarded client fighting to keep custody of his daughter. The excellent performance of Penn cannot be denied (he received an Oscar nomination), but the film is more sentimental than it needs to be and has a premise that strains credibility.

Inherit the Wind (1960)
Directed by Stanley Kramer
Screenplay by Nathan E. Douglas and Harold Jacob Smith

A fictionalized version of the Scopes Monkey Trial, where a high school teacher (Dick York) is charged with teaching Darwin's theory of evolution to his class in violation of state law. Lawyers descend on the small town, including the evangelical Matthew Harrison Brady (Fredric March) defending creationism and civil libertarian Henry Drummond (Spencer Tracy) attempting to clear the teacher. High courtroom drama ensues. Judge Mel, played by Harry Morgan, tries to keep a lid on the grandstanding. A tad didactic, but quite enjoyable because of the topic and the excellent performances of March and Tracy.

Intolerable Cruelty (2003)
Directed by Joel Coen
Screenplay by Robert Ramsey & Matthew Stone, and Ethan Coen & Joel Coen

Suave, fast-talking divorce lawyer Miles Massey (George Clooney) falls for sexy divorcée Marilyn Rexford (Catherine Zeta-Jones), who is hatching a plot of her own to get back at Massey for helping her adultrous ex-husband (Edward Herrmann) get out of their marriage alimony-free. An uneven but still laugh-out-loud farce, where both Clooney and Zeta-Jones appear to love playing it appropriately over the top.

Jagged Edge (1985)
Directed by Richard Marquand
Screenplay by Joe Eszterhas

Glenn Close plays single-mom lawyer Teddy Barnes, who is defending a newspaper editor played by Jeff Bridges, accused of savagely butchering his wife. Teddy falls for the man in the process, but is she in love with a murderer? A mildly interesting mystery-thriller that has not aged particularly well.

JFK (1991)
Directed by Oliver Stone
Screenplay by Oliver Stone and Zachary Sklar

Real life New Orleans District Attorney Jim Garrison (Kevin Costner) attempts to expose the conspiracy to kill President John F. Kennedy, ultimately accusing Clay Shaw (Tommy Lee Jones) of masterminding the plot. The specifics of the conspiracy are outlandish to say the least, but the film manages to be intriguing nonetheless. If even ten percent of the hundreds of facts that Oliver Stone presents about the JFK assassination are true, something was truly rotten on November 22nd in the state of Texas.

Judge Dredd (1995)
Directed by Danny Cannon
Screenplay by William Wisher and Steven E. de Souza

In a post-apocalyptic future, Judge Dredd (Sylvester Stallone) is the most feared of "The Judges," the law enforcers who keep order in a lawless society by acting as police, judge, and jury, pronouncing verdicts on the spot, and executing sentences of culprits they apprehend. Max von Sydow is the Chief Justice. A very interesting premise that quickly degenerates into a run-of-the-mill action film.

The Juror (1996)
Directed by Brian Gibson
Screenplay by Ted Tally

Single mom Annie Laird (Demi Moore) joins a jury, and is soon terrorized by a sinister mob heavy (Alec Baldwin), who threatens her life and her family unless she is able to move the entire jury to a verdict of "not guilty" for the mob boss defendant. Judge Weitzel, played by Michael Constantine, appears to have been compromised by the gangsters as well. The only thing that makes the movie watchable is the charisma of Moore and Baldwin, and even that is not enough to recommend it.

Jury Duty (1995)
Directed by John Fortenberry
Screenplay by Neil Tolkin, and Barbara Williams & Samantha Adams

Slacker Tommy Collins (Pauly Shore) attempts to keep a jury in deadlock so that he can remain housed and fed in sequestration, and continue earning his five dollars a day. The film attempts in vain to be a comedic version of *Twelve Angry Men*. Pauly Shore is a kind of guilty pleasure who, like Jerry Lewis, has to be a little admired for his ability to fully commit to the stupidity and goofiness of his characters. Still, that does not warrant anyone having to subject himself or herself to a viewing of this comedy-without-laughs.

Kramer vs. Kramer (1979)
Directed by Robert Benton
Screenplay by Robert Benton

Ted Kramer (Dustin Hoffman), assisted by his lawyer John Shaunessy (Howard Duff), battles his ex-wife (Meryl Streep) and her lawyer (Bill Moor) for the custody of their young son. Judge Atkins (Howland Chamberlain) presides over the case. An excellent film that has been somewhat forgotten over the years. Completely worthy of the five Academy Awards it received, including Oscars for Hoffman's and Streep's superlative performances.

Laws of Attraction (2004)
Directed by Peter Howitt
Screenplay by Aline Brosh McKenna and Robert Harling

Two divorce lawyers (Julianne Moore and Pierce Brosnan) do ferocious battle in court but eventually fall in love, naturally. A legal romantic comedy that continues the devolution from *Adam's Rib* to *Legal Eagles* to this, the weakest and least entertaining of the bunch. Charming performances all around cannot save the boring script.

Legal Eagles (1986)
Directed by Ivan Reitman
Screenplay by Jim Cash and Jack Epps Jr.

Lawyer Laura Kelly (Debra Winger) defends and District Attorney Tom Logan (Robert Redford) prosecutes a flaky performance artist (Daryl Hannah) accused of stealing a valuable painting that she claims was a gift to her from her father, who was murdered before her eyes when she was a young child. A modern, poor man's *Adam's Rib.*

Legally Blonde (2001)
Directed by Robert Luketic
Screenplay by Karen McCullah Lutz and Kirsten Smith

Sweet airhead Elle Woods (Reese Witherspoon) charms her way into Harvard Law School in order to pursue her shallow boyfriend (Matthew Davis). Elle eventually proves herself as an unconventional but smart lawyer, impressing her professor (Victor Garber), who hires her as an intern at his law firm. A cute, clever, and amusing legal comedy that benefits from Witherspoon's substantial appeal.

Liar Liar (1997)
Directed by Tom Shadyac
Screenplay by Paul Guay and Stephen Mazur

Unscrupulous lawyer Fletcher Reede (Jim Carrey) is forced to tell the truth for one whole day when his young son makes it his birthday wish. Jason Bernard plays the straight man judge, Swoosie Kurtz plays opposing counsel Dana Appleton, Amanda Donohue plays the firm's sexy senior partner, and Jennifer Tilly plays the nasty client seeking a divorce. A fun premise, very well executed by Carrey for some real laugh-out-loud moments.

The Life and Times of Judge Roy Bean (1972)
Directed by John Huston
Screenplay by John Milius

Paul Newman plays the self-appointed "Judge" Bean, a kind of vigilante with the largest Napolean complex in the west. He acts as judge and jury, twisting the law to serve whatever his particular view of justice is at any given moment. A somewhat strange and not very successful tall-tale western, despite a solid performance by Newman.

The Man Who Shot Liberty Valence (1962)
Directed by John Ford
Screenplay by Willis Goldbeck and James Warner Bellah

A lawyer in the old west (James Stewart) finds himself an unlikely hero when he stands up to a gunslinging thug (Lee Marvin). His protector is Tom Doniphon (John Wayne). A good western made better by the charismatic performances of Stewart and Wayne.

Minority Report (2002)
Directed by Steven Spielberg
Screenplay by Scott Frank and Jon Cohen

In a futuristic world, police detective John Anderton (Tom Cruise) can seek out and arrest murderers before they actually commit their crimes, based on the psychic visions of three "pre-cogs" as certified by a judge. Visceral and visually striking, the film takes a thought-provoking scenario and piles on surprising twists and turns, creating a science-fiction masterwork.

Miracle on 34th Street (1947)
Directed by George Seaton
Screenplay by George Seaton

Lawyer Fred Gailey (John Payne) must defend Kris Kringle (Edmund Gwenn) in a sanity case because Kris claims to be the one and only Santa Claus. Judge Harper (Gene Lockhart) balances his dedication to the law with his shortcomings and his humanity. Gwenn remains the only actor to win an Oscar for playing Santa. A magical classic that is all the more satisfying because it presents a completely credible and legally sound argument to substantiate Kris's claims.

Miracle on 34th Street (1994)
Directed by Les Mayfield
Screenplay by George Seaton and John Hughes

An unnecessary remake of the 1947 film of the same name that takes what was sweet in the original plot and ratchets it up to become treacle. The legal argument is substantially weakened as well. The actors are not to be blamed, however, with Sir Richard Attenborough as Kris Kringle, Dylan McDermott as lawyer Bryan Bedford, and Robert Prosky as Judge Harper providing likeable performances along with the amiable supporting cast.

Mississippi Burning (1988)
Directed by Alan Parker
Screenplay by Chris Gerolmo

FBI agents played by Willem Dafoe and Gene Hackman come to the deep south to investigate the murders of some freedom riders during the civil rights movement. The film contains a courtroom sequence exposing how entrenched racism is in this Mississippi community. A powerful and captivating film that manages not to get preachy, thanks to Parker's masterful direction.

Mrs. Doubtfire (1993)
Directed by Chris Columbus
Screenplay by Randi Mayem Singer and Leslie Dixon

Recently divorced father Daniel Hillard (Robin Williams) goes to great lengths to be with his children, even posing as a kindly, old, female housekeeper. He and his ex-wife (Sally Field) eventually battle it out in court á la *Kramer vs. Kramer* in front of a judge played by Scott Beach. While it could easily be mistaken for disposable, high-concept Hollywood fluff, this film is instead a completely amiable, sometimes hilarious family comedy with a tender message, that comes together as a kind of quiet comedic classic.

Murder in the First (1995)
Directed by Marc Rocco
Screenplay by Dan Gordon

A rookie public defender played by Christian Slater tries to clear Henri Young (Kevin Bacon), an inmate of Alcatraz prison, of the murder of a fellow inmate, saying that the inhumane conditions of Henri's captivity, including three solid years in solitary confinement, drove him to kill. R. Lee Ermey plays the erratic judge overseeing the case. Based on the real case that shut down Alcatraz. Despite some very good performances, particularly by Bacon, the film never really rises above mediocre.

Music Box (1989)
Directed by Costa-Gavras
Screenplay by Joe Eszterhas

A lawyer, played by Jessica Lange, defends her father (Armin Mueller-Stahl) when he is accused of being a Nazi war criminal. The evenhanded Judge Silver is played in an understated performance by J. S. Block. Donald Moffat plays another morally ambiguous senior law partner. A vastly underrated drama that keeps the audience guessing until the very end whether the father is guilty of the crimes of which he is accused.

My Cousin Vinny (1992)
Directed by Jonathan Lynn
Screenplay by Dale Launer

Streetwise rookie lawyer Vincent LaGuardia Gambini (Joe Pesci) takes his girlfriend (Marisa Tomei) down south to defend his cousin (Ralph Macchio) and his cousin's friend (Mitchell Whitfield) in a murder trial being conducted in front of the tough Judge Chamberlain Haller (Fred Gwynne). A hilarious comedy that stands up to multiple viewings thanks to great performances (especially Pesci, Gwynne, and Tomei, who won an Oscar for her work) and a clever script.

Nell (1995)
Directed by Michael Apted
Screenplay by William Nicholson and Mark Handley

Doctors played by Liam Neeson and Natasha Richardson are ordered by a judge played by Joe Inscoe to observe a "wild child" (Jodie Foster) and recommend a course of action to the court regarding her mental state and ability to fend for herself. Despite heroic efforts by Foster, the film falls flat.

New Jack City (1991)
Directed by Mario Van Peebles
Screenplay by Thomas Lee Wright and Barry Michael Cooper

A modern gangster tale about the rise of crack cocaine as the drug of choice on the mean streets of Harlem during the Reagan years of the eighties. Lording over it all is the ruthless Nino Brown (Wesley Snipes), who is hauled into court for his drug dealing, only to get off on an easy plea bargain. Van Peebles creates a kind of urban classic that manages to be cautionary without being preachy.

Night and the City (1992)
Directed by Irwin Winkler
Screenplay by Robert Price

A modern film noir with Robert De Niro as a lowlife lawyer trying to make it in the world of small-time boxing promotion. Not only does he fail, he brings down his girlfriend restaurateur (Jessica Lange) by, unbeknownst to her, providing her with a counterfeit liquor license. Solid performances and well written, but so downbeat, one is left to wonder, what is the point?

Nuts (1987)
Directed by Martin Ritt
Screenplay by Tom Topor, and Darryl Ponicsan & Alvin Sargent

Call girl Claudia Draper (Barbra Streisand) is on trial arguing her sanity after killing a murderous client (Leslie Nielsen). She is defended by her tough but caring lawyer Aaron Lewinsky (Richard Dreyfuss). James Whitmore plays Judge Stanley Murdoch. A little melodramatic, but a solid, underrated drama with taut courtroom action buoyed by tremendous performances all around.

The Pelican Brief (1993)
Directed by Alan J. Pakula
Screenplay by Alan J. Pakula

A law student, played by Julia Roberts, unwittingly uncovers the dark secret behind a string of murders of Supreme Court justices. Other lawyers in the film run the moral gamut from the brave corporate whistleblower (Jake Weber as Curtis Morgan) to a scheming murderer (Anthony Heald as Marty Velmano). A silly star vehicle based on another John Grisham novel that cannot rise above its fairly ridiculous plot.

Philadelphia (1993)
Directed by Jonathan Demme
Screenplay by Ron Nyswaner

Successful lawyer Andrew Beckett (Tom Hanks) becomes a client when he is fired from his law firm for being gay and having AIDS. Joe Miller (Denzel Washington), a lawyer best known for soliciting business through his television ads, takes on Andy's case. Jason Robards and Robert Ridgely play senior partners in the firm, and Mary Steenburgen plays the lawyer defending them. Roberta Maxwell plays the judge overseeing the case. Hanks received his first Oscar for his performance. The sober direction comes off a little flat, but the film is still powerful because of its topic: the first big-budget film to tackle both homosexuality and AIDS.

Presumed Innocent (1990)
Directed by Alan J. Pakula
Screenplay by Frank Pierson and Alan J. Pakula

A keeps-you-guessing whodunnit featuring Harrison Ford as Rusty Sabich, the lawyer on trial for the murder of a sexy colleague (Greta Scacchi). Brian Dennehy plays his District Attorney boss, and Raul Julia is Sandy Stern, Rusty's sophisticated and talented defense lawyer trying to prove his client's presumed innocence.

Judge Lyttle (Paul Winfield) has an involvement beyond just presiding over the case. A very satisfying murder mystery with good courtroom action.

Primal Fear (1996)
Directed by Gregory Hoblit
Screenplay by Steve Shagan and Ann Biderman

Shallow, hot-shot lawyer Marty Vail (Richard Gere) defends a young runaway (Edward Norton) accused of violently murdering an archbishop. Marty's former girlfriend (Laura Linney) is prosecuting young Aaron. Alfre Woodard as Judge Shoat runs a tight courtroom. A breakout performance by Norton and a couple of neat surprise twists make the film better than average but still less than great.

The Rainmaker (1997)
Directed by Francis Ford Coppola
Screenplay by Francis Ford Coppola

Fresh out of law school, rookie lawyer Rudy Baylor (Matt Damon) works with bar exam flunkee Deck Shifflet (Danny DeVito) to sue an insurance company that is ripping off their low-income clients. Great star turns by Jon Voight as the high-priced opposing counsel, Leo F. Drummond, Dean Stockwell as the world-weary Judge Hale, Danny Glover in an uncredited role as his replacement, Judge Tyrone Kipler, and Mickey Rourke as the crooked but capable shyster J. Lyman "Bruiser" Stone. A formulaic but still very good drama based on a John Grisham novel about a rookie lawyer getting stripped of his idealism very early in his career. DeVito is particularly good at being both slimy and likeable.

Regarding Henry (1991)
Directed by Mike Nichols
Screenplay by J. J. Abrams

Ruthless lawyer Henry Turner (Harrison Ford) reverts to the intelligence of a five-year-old after being shot in the head, in the process regaining his morality and the love of his family. Donald Moffat plays another of his great roles as the less-than-completely-honest senior partner at the law firm. Nice performances by both Ford and Annette

Bening as his wife, but ultimately it cannot rise above its sentimental, morally simplistic plot—the cinematic equivalent of *Everything I Needed to Know I Learned in Kindergarten.*

Reversal of Fortune (1990)
Directed by Barbet Schroeder
Screenplay by Nicholas Kazan

Ron Silver as real-life rock star lawyer Alan Dershowitz defending tabloid millionaire Claus von Bulow (Jeremy Irons in an amazing, Oscar-winning performance), who is accused of poisoning his wife Sunny (Glenn Close) and putting her in a coma. Clearly based on Dershowitz's account of the events and pumped up by his more-than-healthy ego, the film still tells a fascinating story in a cinematically original way, bolstered by excellent acting by all involved.

Runaway Jury (2003)
Directed by Gary Fleder
Screenplay by Brian Koppelman & David Levien, and Rick Cleveland, and Matthew Chapman

A jury consultant named Rankin Fitch (Gene Hackman), who has been hired to buy a verdict for his gun manufacturer client, is foiled by a con man of sorts named Nicolas Easter (John Cusack), who has made his way onto the jury himself. Dustin Hoffman plays Wendell Rohr, the idealistic opposing counsel. Bruce McGill plays Judge Harkin. Plot twists get a little too cute by half in this film based on a Grisham novel, but the scene allowing two of the great actors of our time—Hackman and Hoffman—go at it with each other justifies the movie all on its own.

The Star Chamber (1983)
Directed by Peter Hyams
Screenplay by Roderick Taylor and Peter Hyams

New judge Steven Hardin (Michael Douglas) is invited by his colleague, Judge Benjamin Caulfield (Hal Holbrook), to join a secret society of judges, who meet in an attempt to compensate for technicalities and loopholes in the law by dispensing vigilante justice of their own. The film's most interesting feature is its premise, and it has little to offer beside that.

Suspect (1987)
Directed by Peter Yates
Screenplay by Eric Roth

Public defender Kathleen Ryan (Cher), assisted by juror Eddie Sanger (Dennis Quaid), attempts to clear a homeless man (Liam Neeson) who has been framed for a murder. An obstinate judge (John Mahoney) seems hell bent on foiling her. A plot that strains credibility prevents this from being much more than a dated, passable star vehicle.

A Time to Kill (1996)
Directed by Joel Schumacher
Screenplay by Akiva Goldsman

Brash young lawyer Jake Brigance (Matthew McConaughey) attempts to defend an African-American defendant (Samuel L. Jackson) who has killed the racists who beat and raped his young daughter. He is assisted by his ethically challenged lawyer friend (Oliver Platt), his lawyer mentor (Donald Sutherland), and a young law student (Sandra Bullock), and opposed by an ambitious prosecutor (Kevin Spacey). The film, another John Grisham adaptation, wallows in cliché, and as a result never quite lives up to its lofty, well-meaning aspirations.

To Kill a Mockingbird (1962)
Directed by Robert Mulligan
Screenplay by Horton Foote

Small-town lawyer and single father Atticus Finch (Gregory Peck) defends a Black man (Brock Peters) wrongly accused of attacking a White girl. Perhaps the greatest of all courtroom films, and one that truly deserves its classic status, in no small part due to Peck's Oscar winning, seminal performance. This is what filmmaking is all about.

Trial and Error (1997)
Directed by Jonathan Lynn
Screenplay by Sara Bernstein and Gregory Bernstein

When a lawyer (Jeff Daniels) is unable to appear in court after his stag party, his actor friend (Michael Richards) tries to pass himself off as a lawyer and impersonate his way through a court case, defending an unscrupulous con man played by Rip Torn. Austin Pendleton as the judge provides some of the few laughs in this otherwise lame courtroom comedy.

True Believer (1989)
Directed by Joseph Ruben
Screenplay by Wesley Strick

A renegade but burnt-out lawyer (James Wood) and his idealistic protégé (Robert Downey Jr.) try to spring a client (Yuji Okumoto) from prison after the young man is framed for murder. Ambitious District Attorney Robert Reynard (Kurtwood Smith) stands in their way. A solid and mostly underrated legal drama.

Twelve Angry Men (1957)
Directed by Sidney Lumet
Screenplay by Reginald Rose

The jurors in a murder trial try to come to a unanimous verdict despite the doubts of Juror #8 (Henry Fonda). Superb ensemble acting and a great gimmick—real-time action that never leaves the jury room—makes this a classic and one of the best legal films ever made.

The Untouchables (1987)
Directed by Brian De Palma
Screenplay by David Mamet

In prohibition-era Chicago, Eliot Ness (Kevin Costner) and his team of agents bring Al Capone (Robert De Niro) to justice, despite a corrupted courtroom environment that includes a tainted judge (Tony Mockus Sr.) and jury. A slick and very entertaining modern gangster film, featuring a memorable performance by Sean Connery as a beat cop turned crusader, and a great turn by De Niro as Capone.

The Verdict (1982)
Directed by Sidney Lumet
Screenplay by David Mamet

A down-and-out alcoholic lawyer, played by Paul Newman, gets a chance to redeem himself with a big medical malpractice case against the archdiocese of Boston. Getting in his way are a lazy judge (Milo O'Shea) and the high-priced lawyer (James Mason) defending the hospital. Well done drama, with Newman's excellent Oscar nominated performance being the high point.

Who Framed Roger Rabbit (1988)
Directed by Robert Zemeckis
Screenplay by Jeffrey Price and Peter S. Seaman

In a 1930s California where humans and cartoons interact, Detective Eddie Valiant (Bob Hoskins) attempts to clear 'toon Roger Rabbit (voiced by Charles Fleischer), who has been charged with murder by the creepy Judge Doom (Christopher Lloyd). Features incredible special effects that are still "how did they do it?" head scratchers, plus such pleasurable moments as seeing Daffy and Donald Ducks battling each other during a piano duet.

Wild Things (1998)
Directed by John McNaughton
Screenplay by Stephen Peters

A popular teacher (Matt Dillon) is accused of sleeping with two of his students (Denise Richards and Neve Campbell), and retains an ambulance-chasing lawyer played wonderfully by Bill Murray to defend him in front of Judge Sylvia B. Waxman (Victoria Bass). A slick and fun, if somewhat ridiculous, murder mystery chock full of surprising plot twists.

The Wrong Man (1956)
Directed by Alfred Hitchcock
Screenplay by Maxwell Anderson and Angus McPhail

The true story of Manny Balestrero (Henry Fonda), a family man who, as the title implies, is wrongly identified as a thief and becomes lost in New York's criminal justice system. An uncharacteristically lackluster performance by Fonda, who maintains a dazed demeanor for way too long, perhaps the entire length of the film. Not one of Hitchcock's best either, but mediocre Hitchcock is still better than most other films.

Notes

1. http://www.imdb.com/ (accessed January 30, 2004).
2. Ron Castell, ed., *Blockbuster Video Guide to the Movies 1995* (New York: Dell Publishing, 1994), xi.
3. American Film Institute, "AFI's 100 Years . . . 100 Heroes and Villains, http://www.afi.com/tvevents/100years/handv.aspx (accessed January 30, 2004).
4. 378 U.S. 184, 197 (1964).
5. Tony Kushner, *Angels in America: A Gay Fantasia on National Themes; Part Two: Perestroika*. New York: Theatre Communications Group, Inc., 1994, p. 110.
6. Thanks to IMDb for this interesting piece of trivia at http://www.imdb.com/name/nm0919583/bio (accessed August 30, 2004).
7. Humphrey Taylor, "Trust in Priests and Clergy Falls 26 Points in Twelve Months," *The Harris Poll* #63 (November 27, 2002), http://www.harrisinteractive.com/harris_poll/index.asp?PID=342 (accessed September 1, 2004).
8. Lisa Fisher, "Survey Reveals Public Perception of Lawyers is Very Low," *The Gainesville Sun*, January 5, 2003.

Index

About the Author

ROSS D. LEVI serves as Legislative Counsel for the Empire State Pride Agenda, New York's statewide gay and lesbian civil rights organization. He has worked in the publicity and promotions departments of Hollywood studios including Miramax, Universal, and 20th Century Fox.